DARE TO BE
AVERAGE

DARE TO BE
AVERAGE

FINDING BRILLIANCE
IN THE COMMONPLACE

Ken Wells, MDiv, MA, LPC, CSAT-S, LISAC

First edition, 2020

ISBN:
Independently published

Cover design by Jody Henning
Interior design by Andrea Reider

Editor's Note: This publication is not intended as a substitute for the advice of health or legal professionals.

Advance Praise for Dare to Be Average

"Having played 12 years in the NBA and been a 3 time NBA All-Star, I know the feeling of not being good enough. Some of that attitude comes from early life experiences. Ken's book unlocks the door to this devastation, and offers insightful information on embracing peace and fulfillment."

—Tom Van Arsdale, former NBA basketball player

"In a world where most are striving to feel they matter; Ken gently and honestly moves the reader through a process to accept the average in life as a way of unlocking individual brilliance. His creative perspective on average moved and challenged me to reflect and contemplate how the average in life is my best teacher."

—Marcus R. Earle, Ph.D., LMFT, CSAT, S-PSB, Clinical Director, Psychological Counseling Services, Ltd.

"My baseline is crazy so for someone to dare me to gamble with my whole life, jump off a cliff without looking is not much of a challenge. I have been self-destructing my whole life, but for Ken Wells to repeatedly dare me to be moderate and average and give me tools to achieve that has brought the greatest joy and peace in my life."

—David Choe, artist

"I have had the privilege of being a friend and colleague of Ken Wells for around 30 years. *Dare to be Average* challenges all of us to be the best we can be and to be comfortable in our own skin. Ken integrates his life experiences into his therapeutic relationship with his clients. No one does a better job than he when it comes to working with others. He is grounded and celebrates the brilliance in everyone. He uses his own pain and joy to challenge us to be open to the *negative*, as well as the *positive* in our lives. He is an invitation to existential depth in terms of spirituality. The evolution of Ken Wells continues to be an inspiration to me and my staff. *Dare to Be Average* will be a new useful tool for therapists and the general public.

—Ralph H. Earle, MDiv, Ph.D., ABPP, LMFT, CSAT, founder and Clinical Director, Psychological Counseling Services

"Ken brings to light a simple, paradoxical, and beautiful idea in *Dare to Be Average*. One that challenges how we derive meaning in our lives. As with all things Ken, he does so in a warm and personal way."

—Kris Keul, MA, LAC

DEDICATION

I dedicate this writing to those folks who feel stuck in average happenings and who have failed to realize that the common place in living is the gateway to inner brilliance.

Contents

Introduction 1

Chapter 1: Destination Average—The Scariest Place on Earth. . . . 7
Chapter 2: What It Takes to Be Average. 25
Chapter 3: Barriers to Realizing Brilliance in Common Places. . . 39
Chapter 4: Four Benefits of Embracing Average 59
Chapter 5: How to Begin—Five Keys to Building
            Your Community 83
Chapter 6: Living with Loneliness and Making It Meaningful . . 103
Chapter 7: Going Deep—Being Your Authentic, True Self. 123
Chapter 8: Going Deep—Embracing Tolerance
            and Forgiveness 131
Chapter 9: Going Deep—Allowing Sorrow to Do Its Work. . . . 145
Chapter 10: Going Deep with the Dread of Obscurity 157
Chapter 11: Going Deep by Coming to Terms with Boredom . . . 169
Chapter 12: Slowing Down and Creating Solitude 177
Chapter 13: Stalking the Shame that Blunts Brilliance 193
Epilogue 215

Appendix 219

Acknowledgments 225
About the Author 227

Introduction

People are always looking for the single magic
bullet that will totally change everything.
There is no single magic bullet.
—Temple Grandin

Stephen, fifty-five, has been married to his wife, Tammy, for fourteen years. Recently, she found texts on his phone of a sexual nature that were sent to a prostitute who offered her services and a hook-up date. This was not the first time he had reached out to prostitutes. As the truth unfolded, it revealed that Stephen had acted out literally hundreds of times before his wife discovered the texts.

Tammy was broken hearted and livid about the destructive behaviors exhibited by her husband. She cried constantly and was hostile toward him. She determined that their fourteen years of marriage was a lie and often screamed profanities at him. In response, Stephen promised to do whatever necessary to heal the marriage (including therapy) and stop the behavior. He was paralyzed with fear and wanted her screaming and constant tears to stop.

1

Stephen began attending Twelve Step meetings with others who exhibited the same behaviors he did. He recruited a sponsor and was determined to go to a counselor who was a specialist in treating this kind of hurtful behavior. The therapist asked him, "What do you want to be different?"

"I want to do whatever it takes to help my wife stop crying about my sexual acting out." He wanted a magic bullet. When asked what it would feel like if he could somehow find a magic bullet that would help her stop crying, he responded, "Well, then I could escape the unbearable guilt and shame that smothers me."

The reality is that in order to heal, both Stephen and Tammy must embrace the deep emotional pain caused by his hurtful behavior. Tammy must face the dreadful pain and, figuratively, "scrub the wound" of betrayal. Temple Grandin is right—there is no magic bullet when it comes to healing the emotional pain of betrayal through infidelity.

In our culture, there is an inbred desire to seek instant relief from physical pain, emotional discomfort, and personal struggle. We tell ourselves that life would be better if we could just find that instant fix! Yet, most times there is no lightning in a bottle. Americans spend billions of dollars on painkillers every year seeking relief from physical pain or attempting to escape the emotional pain derived from mental stress and malady. Likewise, people spend billions of dollars in casinos chasing the dream of finding a financial fix. Today, the number of people who seek escape from the pervading loneliness present in all types of emotional and physical pain through prescribed and street drugs is of epidemic proportions.

We have all read stories of what happened to lottery winners who became instant millionaires. Even the nightmare stories about winners who became losers through mismanaged lives and finances and filed for bankruptcy have little impact on lottery ticket sales. Infomercials advertise schemes, strategies, and concepts that seem to suggest that there is a magic bullet, and if you can understand the secret, it will become a game changer for your financial future. Religion offers its own brand of magic bullet, beckoning folks to participate in faith exercises of all kinds that ultimately promise a magic bullet for heartache and unhappiness.

In my work as a professional counselor, I find that many of my clients hope that the latest technology, therapeutic modality, and pharmacology (including hallucinogens) will rid them of their stress and despair. They desperately reach for anything and everything that will sedate or numb the pain, even when they know relief is temporary and won't work. I often hear comments such as:

"Give me a formula for not worrying."

"Tell me how I can keep my child from overdosing on heroin."

"What kind of medication can I take to keep me from sexually acting out?"

"Give me something to get rid of the picture in my head of my partner being in bed with someone else. It's driving me insane."

Often, when people realize there is no magic cure for such requests, ambition to begin the therapeutic process wanes dramatically. People are sad when I tell them there is no magic bullet. There is no instant fix when sadness descends, life sucks, or you suffer losses. M. Scott Peck[1] was accurate when he said in *The Road Less Traveled* that "life is difficult." It is! Yet, I am grateful that there are plenty of life experiences that can bring peace, joy, and fulfillment.

It is common for people to look for the sensational fix, the spectacular! It's the reason some people are willing to go on national television with celebrity therapists such as Dr. Phil. They are hoping for a magical solution that will take them out of a difficult predicament or painful struggle.

An alternative to a magic bullet is when we embrace life's struggles, lean into painful experiences big and small, and become open to the significance of uninspired moments—the hours of our everyday existence that are ordinary and simple.

Transformation and healing occur not in the spectacular moments under a spotlight of attention but rather in nondescript spaces and places where no one is watching or paying attention. I often hear stories of recovery that are fought and won in the private portals of one's mind and heart. It's a place that no one but you can possibly appreciate because no one is there but you. This counterintuitive approach paradoxically creates fulfillment in life and clarifies meaning and purpose in the presence of pain and discomfort in ways that are missed by those in search of a magic bullet.

Couples such as Stephen and Tammy, who would like to find a magic bullet to avoid the agony and pain that is all around, wallow in the uncertainty and hollow heartache of broken trust. Yet, in the darkest moments when no one is noticing, the change begins. Those seemingly unimportant moments are what I identify as

---

1. M. Scott Peck. *The Road Less Traveled* (New York: Simon & Schuster, 2002), 15.

average places in life. These are mostly overlooked; seen as annoying, unwanted distractions.

Yet most of our days are made up of the routine of common experience. Whether it is freeway traffic, trouble with the IRS, worry about a family member, or a million other common experiences, we all share them. Meaningfulness in life is unpacked when we embrace the customary and commonplace. In the common events and experiences of life, people uncover their own significance. It happens when we reframe the daily grind—the everyday struggles that yield a reason to be and give a "why" to live. Those who are capable of going underneath the average everyday experience begin to uncover one of life's greatest gifts—their own inner brilliance. Inner brilliance distinguishes the extraordinary competence that exists within every human being.

These places are so prevalent to the human condition that I suggest we "dare to be average." Are you ready to explore what it takes to be average? It's more courageous than you might think.

Chapter 1

Destination Average— The Scariest Place on Earth

I'm intimidated by the fear of being average.

—Taylor Swift

t was an August evening more than fifty years ago in a little midwestern farmer's town. From my memory, it was a special night. The team that I played for—the Schilling Stars—was facing the Columbia Machine for the city champion-ship. We each had won our division and were scheduled to face off in the City Series Championship game.

It was best of three. I was selected to pitch the opening game and naturally was excited. I had won all of my games that year, including two no-hitters, in which the other team didn't score any runs. The evening was electric. I just loved playing baseball. Of course, it was Little League, so our coach, Bernie Nale, always played everybody for at least two innings. I was always frustrated when we did not have the best players on the field. I just wanted to win.

Some of the kids only played because their parents made them. During this particular year, there was this kid named Williams. He couldn't care less about baseball. Back in the day of Little League, position players would enthusiastically chatter support for their pitcher between pitches—saying things like "meh, meh swing batter!" If the chatter was weak and I was pitching, I would turn to the field and holler for the players to talk it up for me. Once, when I turned around to yell at all the position players to talk it up, I saw Williams standing in right field with his glove on his head! He had picked a dead dandelion and was blowing the spores, watching them fly away in the wind.

I was pissed. Between innings, I stormed to the dugout and complained to the coach to do something about Williams. Coach told me he would talk to the guy who mowed the field and ask if he would cut the grass a little closer so there would be no dandelions to distract Williams next week!

On this night of the City Series, I was glad that Coach was in my camp and intended to play just the guys who would help us win. I remember the smell of popcorn and the pungent odor of cigar smoke. It was all inviting to me. There was a charge of anticipation in the air as the game began. It was a six-inning game, and we were the visiting team.

When I came out to pitch the final inning, there was a buzz in the air. We were ahead 8–0, and I had a perfect game going—no one had reached base to that point. I'm a lefty and remember feeling really pumped when we got the second out. I knew I could get the last guy out. I don't recall how we got him out, but I do remember being deluged with teammates congratulating me for being "perfecto!"

As I made my way off the field, two people said things to me that changed my life. One adult who I looked up to told me the only reason I pitched a perfect game was because of the defense behind me. His son was the shortstop. The other, my brother Jimmy, said to me, "Beckett (my middle name), you will be a ball-player when you can hit .667 the way I did in American Legion ball."

I remember rolling over in my young mind that no matter what I would do, I could never be good enough. To a young and impressionable mind, it was profound. I had tried so hard to be good, but somehow in my mind, I wasn't, and would never be, good enough. I had won all of the games that I pitched that year yet was not selected to play on the All-Star team. I don't recall anyone else saying much about the game or the season, one way or the other. They may have. But, what stuck were the comments made by the adult and my brother who said some pretty stupid stuff to an impressionable kid.

Things in my inner life began to unravel soon thereafter. I lost my confidence and my way around baseball. Within two years of that game, I had given up playing baseball, believing that my best would never be good enough. Whether I would have ever been a decent player later in life is unknown and not even the point. What mattered is that even when I was perfect in that moment in time—it wasn't enough to be happy with myself. These untimely hurtful remarks shaped my young and naive mind.

I have since been able to sit with the ridiculous absurdity that the idea of perfection brings to the human condition. To keep from being less, I needed to strive to be more and more. There is a certain capitalistic influence that fuels the mentality that more is always better. It drives people to avoid being average at all costs. It underscores that to be of value and significance, you must excel with excellence and transcend those who grovel in mediocrity. I am so thankful that I was exposed to experiences at a young age that eventually helped me to see that this is not true.

I have experienced life to be a mixture of ups and downs, successes and failures, bitter and sweet. It has been a tapestry of highs and lows woven together. Often, the most meaningful moments and deepest wisdom have come from times when I failed. I have since come to see failure as a gift.

I was twenty-one years old, and it was 1971. I spent that summer in Charleston, South Carolina, selling Bible books for the Southwestern Book Company. It was unforgettable. After a full week of sales school in Nashville, Tennessee, a car full of other young hopefuls and I drove all night to reach our destination. We arrived with plans to spend the entire summer in Charleston. We hadn't made prior living arrangements and scrambled to find a place to live. Three of us were dropped off in one area of North Charleston and the others left to live the summer at another distant location.

The three of us had no transportation and nowhere to live. We contacted a local pastor who was very helpful. Amazingly, during that day, we had secured a place to live—a small shack on a deserted dirt road just off Rivers Avenue, a major thoroughfare. We could not get through the front door as the front porch had caved in. We got the first month's rent free because we fixed the front porch. The other two months cost the three of us a total of $50 rent. On that first day, I found a used girl's bicycle that became my form of transportation for the summer.

Each of us had heard stories of other college friends who had made good dough by selling Bible books for the summer. That summer I worked harder than I ever had before or since in my life. Unplanned situations helped me grow and mature. I created memories, not all pleasant, that I have never forgotten.

Most people did not appreciate someone knocking on their door at 8:00 a.m. or 10:00 p.m. or, for that matter, at any time, trying to peddle books. I did that for three months every day except Sunday. I had underestimated the unpopularity of my job. I was bitten by dogs, robbed of money, and had my girl's bicycle stolen three times. I survived on a 99 cent breakfast, a 99 cent 45-ounce strawberry milkshake for lunch, and five Crystal hamburgers for $1 for supper each day that summer.

I thought that if I did what I was told to do, didn't cut corners, and worked my ass off, I would make money. I imagined it would be me laughing all the way to bank in the fall. Well, I did all that I was told. I worked eighty hours a week. I made forty book presentations each day. Yet, I carried home with me a heist totaling $371.41, after expenses, for the thirteen weeks I spent selling Bible books.

Before leaving to sell books in May, I was teased and ridiculed by some of my friends that I was doing something really stupid. They were right. All the promises of laughing all the way to the bank disappeared like clouds in my coffee by the end of the summer. I was disillusioned and devastated to say the least.

While driving back from Charleston to Bethany, Oklahoma, where I was attending college, I reflected back to my earlier days in high school. I was a "C" student in high school. In 1969, I graduated somewhere in the low 300s in a class of about 375 or so. In a mock survey by my business teacher, I was voted least likely to go to college. It happened because of something I saw on a Friday night that I shouldn't have seen. After a basketball game, I saw my business teacher with one of the girls from my class. I caught him putting his hand up her skirt in the front seat of his car.

The next week, when I was screwing around in his class, he came to tell me to knock it off. I told him that if he didn't leave me alone I would tell everyone what I saw him do at the gas station the weekend before. To get back at me, he rigged this survey that really didn't mean anything, yet, I was impressionable. Because of the survey, I felt as if I wouldn't succeed and would never make it into college. Not only did I attend college, I became a graduate. I graduated from college with a 2.2 GPA (out of 4 points), with a bachelor's degree in business administration.

During my first year at Southern Nazarene University, my advisor, the business school department head, told me, "Wells, you won't be anything special. You will be a typical nine-to-fiver." As I started my second year of college, I thought about what he said. I've always had this tremendous drive to prove statements like that wrong. Instead of stopping me, his statement drove me to try to succeed. Upon reflection, there have been many times I wish he had been right.

After a summer of selling Bible books, I was totally burned out that fall. By the end of the semester, I had earned an incomplete in one of my classes, an "Unsatisfactory" grade in another, and achieved two Ds in the other two classes. The grades created an acronym of I. D. U. D. on the grade sheet—which is exactly what I felt like—a total failure!

Failure (as well as success) has been a part of almost every aspect of my life. I have been in recovery from addiction for thirty years. Experiencing failure was a meaningful part of the early days of my life in recovery. The same was true in my professional life. I was a pastor for twenty-five years. I pastored in churches that were very large and cutting edge. Most people there thought of me as successful. I left the large church and ended my church career as the pastor of a small church. I knocked on four-thousand doors to get that church up and running. The result? The church closed because the leaders believed that the betrayals of previous pastoral leaders were too overwhelming for them to offer hope to the community.

I agree with a statement by Aaron Rodgers, the revered Green Bay Packers' quarterback: "I've been to the bottom and been to the top, and peace will come from somewhere else."[2] I've uncovered most of my enriched moments in the everyday average spaces and places of life—not in the spectacular but in times of struggle. In truth, moments of embarrassing failure have offered far more insight than all the successful moments put together.

I have mined more value from the experiences during my college Bible book adventure than most undertakings in my adult life. That summer taught me lessons that I needed to learn about shame, adversity, and facing defeat. Like a pack of wolves chasing me through the woods, shame stalked me throughout that summer.

I tried listening to motivational author Earl Nightingale and his secret to success. In a quest to get the most out of life, I read

---

2. Mina Kimes. "The Search for Aaron Rodgers," *ESPN the Magazine*, August 30, 2017, http://www.espn.com/espn/feature/story/_/page/enterpriseRodgers/green-bay-packers-qb-aaron-rodgers-unmasked-searching.

The Magic of Thinking Big. Nothing seemed to help me avoid the web of shame. No matter what I did, shame stalked me. It told me I did not have what it takes to be successful or survive the summer in Charleston. Yet I did survive, and I did learn to redefine success. There were many days that I did not sell any books, even though I tried really hard. I learned what shame felt like and tasted it each Sunday when we would go to a sales meeting and put our numbers on the board for other guys to see. My results sucked!

Even though shame seemed to stalk me, I learned some important lessons about intimacy. The highlight of my summer selling Bible books was a little mixed-breed terrier who would sleep on our front porch. He would wait for me in the morning and follow me as I pedaled my bicycle out to my territory. When I got to my first house, he knew it was time to leave, and he would disappear. I would not see him until the next day. He was the only consistent, predictable sentient being in my life that summer. And he became a source of comfort.

Truth was, he was my only friend all summer long. When I would get off my bike and whistle for him to come to me so that I could pet him, he would come within an arm's reach and then give in to anxiety and fear. He would tuck his tail between his legs and back away. I would start the process all over again. Oddly, though he followed me every day that summer, he never once allowed me to pet him. He was so close yet so far away.

That dog has become a hallowed memory and metaphor that I have cherished and reflected upon throughout my adult years. All the stretch and strain to be the best at what I do and the willingness to pay the price no matter what takes a distant backseat to the insight I gained from this canine companion of so many years ago. How many times have I longed to be loved by someone I wanted to be close to but backed off for fear of abandonment and rejection? That little dog has reminded me that if I want to experience the depth and richness of friendship, I must take the risk of becoming emotionally naked and let that individual touch my spirit of vulnerability.

I discovered this life-giving insight not in the spectacular places of life but in humble spaces filled with dread, fear, and loneliness. These are the average places in which we all engage in one way or another. Rather than overlook them, I have cherished the insights that have surfaced by embracing these average everyday experiences in life. Disappointment and suffering add richness and soulfulness to average mundane moments that otherwise go unnoticed—even discounted and assigned to the category of "ho-hum." I will even go so far to say that these commonplace, average experiences become the soil of life that grows and develops one's own sense of brilliance.

Brilliance in an Average Day to the Average Guy

Every day's an average day—each day we learn to grieve—
People in a hurry—with every day scurry—
runnin' from feelings packed on their sleeve—

Every day's an average day—galvanized with hello and
    good-bye
Mixture of sweet with plenty of bitter
A tapestry of paradox that begs for surrender

I wanna say it straight when people hate
To hear we all got a destiny date
Cause we gonna die, no matter how much you wonder why
'Bout what happens on the other side
Hello today—Good-bye tomorrow
Ain't no place to hide
Gotta learn to grieve, hug the sorrow
It's an average day to say hello—tomorrow, it'll be good-bye

—KEN WELLS

What It Means to Be Average

Failure is a feared word in our culture. Yet, so too, is the idea of being average. The fear of being average is common. Music icon Taylor Swift once shared she was intimidated by the thought of being average. The word is often used as a tool of evaluation and assessment. We use the word to judge whether people are good enough. It becomes a way to separate the masses from those who excel.

In this context, to be average is to be not good enough. It suggests that someone will need to put in more effort to become excellent, elite, or rated Number One in their endeavor. *Average* describes those who are in the middle of the pack. In our society, there is pressure to excel, to achieve, to be a winner, and to avoid being a loser. Accomplishment becomes everything.

In many corridors of life, if you do not rise above average, your value is diminished and you matter less. Significance is too often determined by who has achieved the most.

Historically, the bell-curve grading system has contributed to competitiveness among students. The average score was something to avoid. Average paved the way to determine winners and losers in the classroom. Winners received the higher grades and losers the lower grades. The average grade was the watershed measurement for what to avoid.

In the world of professional sports, if a player is average he is often forgotten and unknown to most fans. For example, Josh McCown, has been what many in football would describe as a journeyman. He has played on twelve professional teams in his sixteen-year career. He has never been a sustained starting quarterback. Essentially, his career is defined as a career back-up quarterback. Yet, the number of years he has played in the NFL is greater than many designated franchise quarterbacks in the league. He has outlasted most. His long tenure is overshadowed by the fact that he has never been the consistent number one quarterback for any team. He would be dubbed as an "average" NFL quarterback.

Many people have been taught to avoid being average. Even though only a few will achieve the evaluation of being outstanding and far more of us will be evaluated as average, it is an assessment that people are taught to avoid like the plague. To be average is to fail. For many, there is the mentality that a "C" grade is like flunking. Some students respond to an A- as if it were an F. The emphasis upon elite accomplishment is extreme in our culture. There is no room for mediocrity, even though President Abraham Lincoln is credited to have said, "God must have loved the common man, he made so many of them."

In our culture, the mundane, insignificant moments of life are often glossed over as unimportant in order to get to the moments of spectacular exhilaration. The message we give our children is that only by achievement are you special. The emphasis is to achieve and accomplish something that will trigger others to say you are special and that you matter. Yet, at some point, so many find that they can never achieve enough to get enough outside validation to fill their needy heart. Even when people get tired of achieving and exhausted with competing for it, they can get stuck in not being able to get enough of what they really don't want. Average becomes a dreaded curse for people trapped in a world of performance.

Average is far more significant to the existence of life than the highest of achievements. There is only one Super Bowl winner among thirty-two NFL teams. While it is admirable to achieve a championship, it is necessary to create meaningfulness in the experience of all the players of the thirty-one teams who did not win. The championship team remains a champion only for a short time.

Even if we are elite, we all have so many common threads of average in other parts of life. Average, commonplace experiences define the human landscape. Hall of Fame pitcher Catfish Hunter said it right when he declared, "The sun don't shine on the same dog's ass all the time." Most asses that get too much sun get sunburned or begin to wither and dry up from the sun's intensity. That's what happens to folks who only live in the spotlight.

It is a mistake to focus on the word *average* only as a tool to evaluate performance. If you expand the word to include commonplace, mundane moments and garden-variety happenings in life, you can identify a different, even deeper application of the word. Average speaks to the mainstream everyday experience of life. It embraces the unremarkable, "white bread" times that connect to everyday existence. It beckons a call from within to a deeper and richer life experience that separates from and supersedes outside scrutiny.

Whether celebrity or commoner, meaningfulness in life is determined less by *doing* and more by embracing *being*. Some folks get restless believing they have to be doing something or always making something happen in order to become the best version of themselves. Social activist Grace Lee Boggs once said that "being is becoming." She believed that life needs to be acted upon in order for change to happen.

Human struggle is a commonplace, average experience that most try to avoid, escape, or deny. Yet struggle is a universal connecting point and a gateway to brilliance. For example, when it comes to treating sexual addiction, I will listen to someone talk about the agony and struggle with sexually objectifying another person. It's not just one person, but it can happen throughout the day, without the capacity to stop. Yet, on other days it might not happen at all, or the trigger to objectify might show up in a different way.

As I listen to these stories of agony, I often hear, "Do you have any idea what this struggle is like inside?"

I tell them that what they are going through is pretty average to the everyday experience of a sex addict. These are the private, lonely, commonplace struggles that an addict faces on any given day. Strong cravings for drugs of choice are common no matter what the drug is. Powerful withdrawal from the substance or mood-altering experience is commonplace for those in the world of addiction recovery. It is an everyday struggle of temptation that is experienced around addictive craving.

When addressed with restraint, an addict can sit with the experience and uncover a legitimate need that must be met in a healthy way. In this way, an addict can transform a curse (addictive use) into a blessing by fulfilling an intimate need in a healthy way.

Sitting with discomfort produces the brilliance of meeting one's need in the moment.

The struggle for honesty is another common thread significant to addiction recovery. The struggle to be honest with self and others is not confined to only an addict's world. Deep emotional honesty is one of the great challenges that confronts us all.

Struggle shows up in a myriad of other ways. Some people struggle with physical or emotional pain. Many battle with the pain and financial stress. Grieving the loss of loved ones, opportunities, friendships, and life itself is a part of the average everyday experience of living. It's helpful to recognize the value of embracing struggle. Dark nights of the soul are classic to all. We are all on a pilgrimage in life that calls for unraveling understanding and meaningfulness in the places where we struggle.

Failure is an average experience of humanity. Because it is painful, we often avoid the discomfort by not admitting our failures and refusing to talk about them. Since the pain of daily struggle is an average experience, learning to lean into it and sit with the discomfort is one way to connect with others who are going through similar circumstances. Rather than resist the emotional experience that comes with any degree of failure, embrace the unwanted feelings and learn to accept them. This act alone turns an average experience into a source of common humanity that strengthens and reinforces resolve.

Michael Jordan was once challenged by his Hall of Fame basketball coach Phil Jackson. He was told in order for his team to be more successful, he would need to accept the limits of allowing the game to come to him instead of trying to force positive outcomes. Michael Jordan did just that—he learned to accept struggle in the game and to allow the game to come to him. It was at this point in his career that he became one of the greatest basketball players of all time.[3]

Acceptance of failure is like the swimmer who stops fighting the water and instead learns to relax and rely upon the water for buoyancy. When the average experiences of human failure are embraced, they become rich moments of insight, understanding, and transformation.

Average becomes the place for all to gain wisdom delivered through life circumstance. In moments of discomfort, we develop insight and life savvy. Many want to alter the state of unhappiness before taking time to listen to the message. So we find a way to numb or medicate the unwanted feeling with food, substances, or experiences that will help us to disconnect from the discomfort. We look outside for a solution when the universe would beckon that we come home, be true to our heart, and allow the average experience to teach its magic about what is meaningful in a pressure-packed world.

For an addict, an average experience would be to avoid uncomfortable and unwanted feelings. When faced with everyday struggles such as the stress that comes from failure, loss, and multiple sources of disappointment, the addicted crave to escape and numb out. The reason is simple. Addiction delivers what it promises every time. The addict may need a higher dose or to take a greater risk, but satisfying the craving delivers what he or she is looking for. Addicts are constantly tempted to ignore limitations and go outside their boundaries to find relief from anxiety and discomfort.

---

3. Paul David Walker. "Are You Chasing Life or Letting it Come to You?" *Huff-Post*, September 13, 2009, updated November 17, 2011, https://www.huffpost.com/entry/are-you-chasing-life-or-1_b_258149.

Metaphors for addiction are all around us. I grew up in east central Illinois. To go home, I often fly from Phoenix to St. Louis. From the airport, I take Interstate 270 around the city of St. Louis leading to the bridge over the Mississippi River that parallels the old Chain of Rocks Bridge that has been shut down and abandoned for decades. After crossing the Mississippi on a parallel bridge, immediately there is another bridge that goes over a canal built for commercial barges to navigate safely through the Chain of Rocks.

The canal is designed to be wide enough to accommodate the barge traffic with a steep shoreline. It is plenty deep so that commercial traffic can navigate with no problem. For me, this canal channel is a metaphor to recovery. There is no danger of the barge becoming impeded or stuck in shallow waters. The canal is designed and properly sized for typical commercial barge traffic. Within its confines, each barge is safe from the hazard of shallow waters.

As long as addicts stay within the confines of healthy boundaries and respect limitation, they are safe from the hazards that lead to addictive acting out. It's only when an addict ignores limitations that he or she gets into trouble with addictive acting out.

I often hear complaints from sexual addicts who resent the need for limitation and boundary. This resistance is an average dynamic experience of most addicts. Yet, true to the metaphor, the individuals who honor and respect limitation will discover that they can go as deep within the boundary as they want. It's by respecting our limits and going deep within the heart that we have the opportunity to know ourselves best.

Canadian poet Shane Koyczan declared that, "To discover the thing you're brilliant at you first have to endure realizing all the things you're average at."

Questions

1. What does "average" look like for you?

2. What experiences can you think of that are "average" that you do every day?

3. Do you have what it takes? Take a moment to reflect on a time when you were judged as average. Did you feel like a failure or not very special? Find someone who is safe to share what the experience was like.

4. It has been said that "life is meant to be lived forward but can only be understood backward." When you look back at when you were judged as average, what did you learn about yourself?

5. When attempting to avoid being labeled as average, did you ignore your own limits and ultimately hurt yourself?

6. What do you think might have happened if you stayed within your limits? What might you have learned from that?

Chapter 2

What It Takes
to Be Average

*Figuring out how to transform everyday, average
experience into sacred space is the beginning point
toward mining personal brilliance.*

—Anonymous

Knowing and understanding the common place of average
everyday living is the touchstone toward uncovering the
magic of your personal brilliance. The corridors of everyday living lead to the rooms that contain personal brilliance. Yet,
the doors of those rooms will never be unlocked and opened
unless you practice transforming meaningfulness into everyday
life experience with an open heart.

Open and Closed Hearts

An open heart is the opposite of a closed heart. A closed heart hides behind a wall of fear and avoids vulnerability. Our hearts become closed when we are harboring shame and don't want to fail. People with closed hearts are defensive, judgmental, and shortsighted. A closed heart fuels pessimism, which can undermine optimism and spontaneity.

An open heart is porous and real, which is most necessary to forge personal brilliance. An open heart connects with the present moment and extracts meaningfulness from commonplace experiences.

Closed-hearted people tend to rivet their focus on outcomes. Life becomes about winning or losing, which is a zero-sum mentality. For example, when I sold Bible books, I recall the extreme pressure I put on myself to make a sale. The more focused I was on selling the books, the more my heart seemed to close and the harder it was to knock on the next door. My closed heart permeated my appearance and presentation. I recall the tears I held back as I went from door to door. I had such a closed heart that I couldn't give the books away. During one week, I had not sold one book and it was Wednesday. I made forty presentations every day for three days and I was 0 for 120! That's a profound slump in anybody's game.

On that same Wednesday, I approached a woman who lived in a mobile home. She identified herself as a Satanist. She was so opposed to the Bible books she told me she cast a curse on me so that I wouldn't sell any books. Since I had already gone three days without selling anything, I figured that I had already been snake bit, so her curse didn't mean much to me.

As fate would have it, I stumbled onto the porch of Mrs. Gilley. She lived in the last house I visited on that most difficult day. She was a retired school teacher who I later learned had been watching me all afternoon going from door to door in her neighborhood. When I brought my closed heart to her front porch, she greeted me with an open heart of absolute total acceptance.

Before I could give her my introductory spiel, she opened the door and whisked me into her home. She already had a check made out for the $45.80—the amount that the entire library cost at that time. She told me to keep the books and give them to some other family. She said she suffered from cataracts and could not read and did not believe in God anyway.

She insisted that I sit down for a dinner that she had prepared just for me. She wouldn't take no for an answer. I don't recall when I had ever been so famished. I left with my stomach so full. My stomach wasn't the only thing that was filled; so too was my heart. This little woman's kindness and spirit opened my heart to the possibility of transforming an average moment of discouragement and failure into the unknown promise of an open heart.

It would be nice to share that I left Mrs. Gilley's home and went on an inspired hot streak of sales. But I didn't. I struggled the entire summer with dismal results. Yet the struggle, discouragement, and failure I had come to know so well became the common ordinary experiences that curated my heart toward finding meaningfulness in a mundane common place. Rather than run away or hide from the failure that was so painful, I learned to sit with the experience. I opened my heart by embracing the unwanted feelings of perceived failure and despair. By doing so, I generated hope for tomorrow.

It was so paradoxical. Facing the embarrassment of defeat and failure enabled me to transform the feelings of shame into compassion for myself and others. It empowered me to gather meaningful insight and wisdom before moving forward and letting go of disappointment and discomfort.

Everybody must face the hurt and heartache of defeat and failure at some point. Those who practice the discipline of embracing the emotional discomfort that always comes with failure have positioned themselves to tap into their personal brilliance.

Open and Closed Hearts Show Up
When You Least Expect Them

An open heart is necessary to create merit out of an ordinary experience. It is sometimes surprising who shows up with an open heart and whose heart is closed. For example, one of my older brothers, Jimmy, joined the Marine Corps and spent thirteen months in Vietnam. After his tour of duty, he returned home and began his professional work. About one year later, he was diagnosed with terminal stage 4 cancer that within eighteen months took his life. Like thousands of other GI's who fought in the war, Jimmy had been exposed to Agent Orange, a lethal defoliate. It happened when his superiors ordered him and others to take baths in the barrels that had previously contained the defoliate.

During his chemotherapy treatment, Jimmy was in total misery. He would vomit for hours, even throwing up bile from his liver. It was intense pain. The chemotherapy put the cancer in remission. He improved but then later the cancer accelerated and Jimmy became more desperate. When Jimmy was really sick, he was staying at our mom and dad's house. One of the church elders promised to come by and pray with Jimmy for healing. It was a really big deal to Jimmy because he was desperate and suffering severe pain.

When the elder arrived, he shared a brief prayer and spent the rest of the time trying to sell Jimmy a set of Shaklee supplements and vitamins. He told Jimmy that he could make monthly payments, and the supplements would help heal his cancer. Everyone knew that in a few months Jimmy would be dead. I recall the cold disappointment Jimmy felt when the elder left. He was so hopeful that somehow God would work a miracle. But, this "servant of God" showed up with his own agenda. The only thing he offered, in addition to the costly supplements, was a closed heart.

On another occasion, Jimmy's old high school baseball buddy Marty Pattin dropped by to see him. Marty had become a bona fide major league baseball pitcher. He established himself in the starting rotation of the Boston Red Sox and at the time was playing for the Kansas City Royals. When Marty came by, he brought two beers, one for him and one for Jimmy to enjoy. They sat around and reminisced about playing ball together. They shared all kind of stories. They laughed and had a lot of fun for about an hour. When Marty left, Jimmy's body still hurt, and he was in no better condition. But his spirit had been lifted, and he experienced relief from fear and distraught for at least that one hour. This happened because Marty showed up with an open heart. There was no closed heart agenda.

I often reflect on those two different visitors. The one who identified as a representative of God from the church had a closed heart, while his old buddy presented an open heart that provided soothing relief for a short period of time. In this ordinary moment of suffering, I witnessed the brilliance and healing of an open heart and the wilting of promise and hope from a closed heart. Brilliance can show up in the least expected places from the least likely people.

What Open-Hearted Living Looks Like

Recovery from any addiction demands an open heart. Recovery requires becoming emotionally naked. Most addictions require a full and complete disclosure. Long-term healing requires open-hearted living every day. Finding purposefulness and importance in everyday mundane moments in life depends upon the capacity to tell on yourself. When unwanted feelings of anxiety, frustration, and disappointment surface, you can share with others what is going on inside rather than bury the feelings. Sometimes, it is helpful to journal feelings and experiences. It is important to share with another and to purposely be connected to a community of support.

Telling on yourself invites you to live with an open heart with no secrets. An open heart allows for every moment that is ordinary to become sacred. The average moment is the common thread that connects people in any given community. In recovery, when I resist and close my heart, I become isolated without the insulation of a community of support. This increases the vulnerability and likelihood of acting out.

Don't Force It

Embracing average means you have cultivated the capacity to allow life to flow to you rather than going after it and forcing things to happen. When I notice myself trying to force things to happen, I know I'm not embracing the wisdom that average spaces in life can bring. While there are times when it is important to make things happen, pushing toward an end result is usually not sustainable. For example, forcing a romantic encounter usually will blow up in your face. Trying too hard to get a job can be a form of self-sabotage.

When we take the time to find meaningfulness in our average experiences, we are usually pulled toward a higher standard of performance and excellence in behavior. We gain clarity on why we do what we do in the average place. When my action is pure and selfless, then things begin to settle into their perfect place, and the energies of life pull me into a passion for everyday living.

There is a phenomenon that happens when I keep pushing for more and more. I never get enough. When I try to fill the empty hole in my soul by pushing for more accomplishment and attainment, I become like a child who cannot get enough sugar. The achievement is never deeply satisfying unless I embrace the journey along the way. It's the journey of the common, mundane everyday experience that creates fulfillment and happiness. Many have embraced a popular mantra about there being no way to happiness because happiness is the way. Embracing happiness includes all the average life experiences that have accumulated along the way. If I don't embrace this understanding, then when I achieve the spectacular it will not be enough or fulfilling.

So many have sighed with dissatisfaction, "Is this all there is?" When I accomplish a goal and do not embrace meaningfulness in the process, then I don't repeat the success or inspire new visions for future goals. It's all contingent on finding happiness and fulfillment in the average everyday pursuit of life. Those who wake up every morning ready to seize the day knowing why they should value the everyday moments are the people who pull through struggle and the disappointment of failure.

Letting life come to you is a Zen mentality necessary to experiencing value in the ordinary, average spaces of life. The goal is to eliminate the need for striving. When I find myself striving, I am clutching and grasping for that which I do not have. While I have seen this approach yield positive results in the short term, it is not sustainable for the long term. It's like the little boy who loved peanut butter and jelly sandwiches. Each day he would go to the kitchen and get his jar of jelly and peanut butter and make his favorite sandwich. When he could see daylight at the bottom of his peanut butter jar, he would chuck the jar in the trash and reach for a new jar from the pantry. However, one day when he reached for a new jar, there was no jar. Disappointed, he walked away knowing he would not have his favorite sandwich.

His father noticed what had just occurred, stopped the little boy, and brought him back into the kitchen. He took the jar out of the trash, wiped it off, removed the lid, and scraped the sides of the jar so that the little boy now had one-half inch of peanut butter rather than his usual one-inch thickness. He then slapped the bread with jelly and the little boy had his favorite sandwich. His father said, "Hey, you were ready to walk away without anything. If you just would have taken the extra time to scrape out the jar, you would have had enough for a sandwich."

I think of this little boy often. So many people become disgruntled with the average mundane experience of life that they throw away its value. They want the full jar of peanut butter. They try winning the lottery, fantasize about the rich and the famous, or daydream about being somewhere, anywhere other than where they are at. If we embrace the average everyday struggle, take what it is, and spread it around, we will make it more. Happiness is not found in the spectacular. It's in how we work with average circumstances.

Gratefulness and Grateful Living

Letting life come to you fosters grateful living. When you master gratefulness, you create an energy source that pulls you through the mundane as you learn to appreciate it. Appreciation of everyday struggles provides the necessary fuel to guide you and deepen the richness of everyday life. Grateful living takes what is and makes it more, simply by the way in which you frame and focus your life circumstance. It fuels motivation—not always to do more but to go deeper into what life is all about.

Gratefulness fuels hunger for deeper understanding and cultivates a "beginner's mind and attitude." It is easy to become complacent and then feel entitled to privilege and spaces of status and power and attainment. Life is not about entitlement. Rather, life is a precious gift to be treasured each and every day with sacred reverence.

Entitled people resemble the classic storyline from the Rocky Balboa movies. The famous boxer came from nothing and with hunger and a "beginner's mind" he worked his way to becoming a champion. Once a champion, he lost focus on the happiness of the journey, which involved arduous training and conditioning. He was out of shape and lowered his standard of excellence that comes from doing what hungry achievers do in average spaces of everyday living. His eventual downfall was his attitude of entitlement.

Gratefulness is not about accomplishment; it's about the journey along the way. It's about what others overlook and discount.

It's about the average, day-in, day-out training and drudgery that creates a champion. It's not about the championship, which is experienced for a fleeting moment, even for the greatest champions. Rather, it is about appreciation for the journey, the average everyday existence that connects a champion, or a wannabe, to the whole world. It's about letting the flow of life take you to a compelling vision that pulls you into the moment of appreciation and understanding of the meaningfulness of average. These are the moments that the mojo, the magic, the brilliance in someone's life comes forward and blossoms.

Embrace the Brokenness

Working through addiction or any other serious difficulty means we must embrace the painful broken places of our lives. It is one thing to read or hear about the inspirational road to recovery in the life of another. It is yet another to begin the walk ourselves. It always leads to the point of most pain—the place of failure. It's like hiking around the mountain looking for the easy way up. It always comes back to the trailhead of facing the pain of failure and discomfort. This chases many people away from recovery. Some say that until the pain of addiction becomes great enough that the addictive behavior is no longer worth it, folks will stay stuck in their addiction. There's no real reason for change. The average place for those facing failure is embracing the brokenness of life.

In my work, I encourage people to scrub the wound of defeat and failure. I talk about leaning into the place of pain. If you do not scrub the wound, it will later fester and infect future behavior with the pus of bitterness, self-sabotage, and reenactment of hurtful traumatic experience. These are the average experiences that are true for anyone who wishes to find meaningfulness in failure. Not scrubbing the wound is like having a fire break out and destroy one room of your house, closing the door on that room, and pretending the charred room doesn't even exist.

When I was young, my mother had a serious accident at home. The pilot light had gone out on the stove. While she was attempting to light the pilot with a match, the gas was leaking out. When she struck the match, fire exploded in her face. She put the fire out on her own but paid a dear price, suffering third-degree burns on her body. I remember the smell of burnt flesh and hair. I watched my mom's face swell into one big blister.

At the time, her parents, who lived close by, rushed over to help her get to the hospital. My grandfather stayed in the car and would not come into the house. It turns out he had lost my mom's sister, Aileen, to fire in a tragic accident when she and my mom were playing with candles as small children. Etched in his memory was the sight of that tragic accident, and he did not want to see the result of my mom's accident.

My grandpa did not want to go back into that charred room where all the damage was done and the pain exists. He did not want to relive his daughter's death from so many years ago. We will go to great lengths to avoid scenes of painful struggle. For those of you who want to work through and go beyond the failure, it is imperative that you open the door, walk into the destroyed room, and sit in the middle of the charred remains to grieve the reality of what took place. You need to figure out how it happened and determine what the next best course of action is to heal the brokenness and to work toward never allowing it to happen again.

This approach is painful but powerfully healing. Embracing devastation allows us to tell ourselves the truth about what happened and leads us through to the other side, where peace, serenity, and joy reside.

The difference is between choosing to embrace the devastation or wallow in it. Embracing the common components of human failure includes showing up vulnerable, accepting what you are responsible for, and courageously taking steps to address the issue while feeling shaky tender about the failure.

As a therapist, I see many people who have suffered great defeat due to their addictive acting out behavior. Some of them refuse to sit in the charred remains. They live the rest of their lives running from the shame of their destructive behavior or are intimidated by the judgment from others about what they did. Meanwhile, those who are willing to embrace this average place of experience in failure find a way to transform their addiction from a curse to a blessing.

For me, how I deal with devastation is critical to cultivating inner brilliance. When I lean into understanding this common experience of pain, I create insight and depth about who I am. I add depth and breadth to my life experience. I can create compassion toward myself and others by embracing the reality of devastation. In this context, I have the power to transform the curse of failure into a blessing of understanding and purposefulness. I can even shift the energy of hate to work toward my most loved and desired result. My weakness, then, becomes my strength.

An old saying that has been quoted by many speaks to being average: "Phony plays for a while, but genuine plays for a lifetime." Precious few of us have never "played phony." All of us in some way have been or are inconsistent, incongruent, and hypocritical. For example, there are certain foods I know to eliminate from my diet or to moderate if I am going to be healthy. Yet, I've sabotaged myself over and over again. Or, I know to work out every day, but I find it difficult to follow through.

Incongruence sets addicts up to live a double life. It occurs when I identify clear values that I want to live my life by. Yet, I have feelings that are very different from the values I embrace. Further, I say things that are at odds with what I feel and thoughts I value. Then, I do things that are contrary to what I think, feel, and say. This typifies the incongruent life of an addict.

Hypocrisy is another average experience of human failure. Some people say they do not go to church because the people there are hypocrites. In response, I have often said, "Duh, do you think? Do you know anyone in any setting who is not hypocritical in some way?" I say to others with great conviction that everyone should start their day with exercise and go for a run early in the morning. Yet, on any given day, you might ask me, "Did you run this morning, Ken?"

I might say, "No, I slept in. I was too lazy to get up." I believe we all have some form of hypocrisy that we have to deal with in an honest moment.

The goal in addressing the average experience of hypocrisy or failure is not to strive to be perfect by avoiding failure. It's not about trying to be more to keep from being less. Rather, the goal is to be accountable to others during average everyday experiences. Your accountability partner will hold your feet to the fire to get you to change your behavior, make a course correction, or make amends and restitution for average everyday acts of human failure. They won't let you wallow in selfish defeat.

If you want to be average, you need to show up every day with a genuine commitment to accountability. You need to be willing to call yourself out when you are inconsistent, incongruent, and hypocritical. Being genuine beckons for a resurrection in human brilliance that comes from a commitment to ongoing change housed in the capsule of humility.

Questions

1. Describe a time when you felt a lot of outside pressure to achieve a certain result that triggered a "closed heart" response from you. Note: the best way to recognize a "closed heart" response is to focus on when you were feeling defensive, judgmental, and shortsighted.

2. Describe an experience in your life similar to the little boy and the peanut butter jar, when you needed to take what was and spread it around and make it enough. How did it feel to shift from a close-hearted response to an open-hearted solution?

3. In what ways have you embraced the experience of failure, or "scrubbed the wound"?

Chapter 3

Barriers to Realizing Brilliance in Common Places

I'm on a drug. It's called Charlie Sheen.
It's not available. If you try it once, you will die.
Your face will melt off and your children
will weep over your exploded body.

—CHARLIE SHEEN

I remember watching Charlie Sheen on *20/20* when he said, "I just didn't believe I was like everybody else. I thought I was unique." The public self-destruction and demolition of Charlie Sheen was painful to follow in the news. The descent from being the highest paid American television actor on a primetime show ($1.8 million per episode on *Two and a Half Men*) to being HIV positive and suspected of threatening to kill a former fiancée all was very sad to his most loyal fan base.

Addiction is all consuming. Brilliance is lost to the twisted, distorted perspective that says, "I am the essence of brilliance." Audacious self-importance keeps a person stuck. Now in reported recovery, Sheen may well speak from a different place than he once was.

There are many examples of people who with a prima donna makeover squelch the possibility of finding importance in connecting with everyday experiences. Addicts miss the connection by being too self-absorbed. There's no time or room for noticing brilliance in the mundane average moment. In their mind, mundane is boring, uncomfortable, and to be avoided at all cost. Instead, arrogance dominates, not only for actors but potentially for anyone. All addicts can act like prima donnas when dominated by a "I want what I want when I want it" mentality. This mind-set renders it impossible to recognize brilliance in the average everyday moment, whether one is an out-of-control addict or somebody else caught up in their own importance.

Before looking at the barriers to discovering our inner brilliance, let's look at what brilliance is and why it's worth the effort. For starters, we are all unrepeatable miracles of the universe. In the book *I-Thou*, Martin Buber wrote, "Every person born into the world represents something new, something that never existed before, something original and unique." This something is wrapped up in the essence of inner brilliance. Brilliance is a fundamental quality of being human. The very nature of human existence begs for splendor and magnificence. Brilliance is the divine uniqueness within that goes much deeper and is more distinct than parental imprint. It is our higher self. It becomes elevated through a deepened understanding of self—which, as you know by now, happens in life's average moments. Brilliance is the unknown creative source within that transforms grasping and greed to giving and loving. We begin to believe in ourselves. It keeps us humble knowing we aren't more brilliant than anybody else—we all have the energy within to know and express our higher self.

The expression of brilliance is as varied as the stars in the universe. Every form of brilliance expressed is unique and unrepeatable. Sometimes brilliance is obvious, like the work of a rocket scientist or great mathematician. Other forms of brilliance are overlooked, such as when a mother intuitively nurtures and comforts her child at the right time. I have witnessed the brilliance of a single mother, who, drawing from her inner wisdom and resilience, offered guidance to her children with amazing insight and moxie. I have sat with elders and listened to the unique brilliance shared about ways to manage limitation, worry, relentless pain, and sorrow.

Our individual brilliance is only limited when we compete and compare it to someone else's intellect, talent, status, or other observable behavior. This is the criteria most people use to measure brilliance. There is never a need to compete with the brilliance of others, only to connect with your own. A zero-sum mentality, doing versus being, a rule-breaker's mentality, and egotism get in the way of embracing and cultivating our inner brilliance. Let's look at each of them.

Barrier #1—A Zero-Sum Mentality

If you look at the developments in the international scene over the past many years, we haven't been able

to resolve many problems and many crises, because we
have approached them from a zero-sum perspective. My
gain has always been defined as somebody else's loss, and
through that, we never resolve problems.

—MOHAMMAD JAVAD ZARIF

Zero-sum mentality impacts many aspects of the world in which we live. In principle, zero-sum living depends upon winners and losers. One person's gain or loss is predicated on the loss or gain of others. It is like taking a larger piece of cake and reducing the amount of cake available to others.

Even the word *brilliant* can bring about a zero-sum influence. When someone produces winning results, we usually try to find some degree of brilliance in it. On the other hand, when someone produces losing results, we often point to what is wrong with their performance. For example, an Olympic hopeful achieves a world record in a swim competition and is bested by one-thousandth of a second on the same day by another competitor. His swim coach focuses on the second-place swimmer's insufficient turns. In this example, the performance of the Olympic hopeful who swam a brilliant unprecedented race was overshadowed by a competitor who was an eyelash faster. The Olympic hopeful can easily lose sight of his own brilliance by comparing himself with his competitor.

What can be easily overlooked is the clever intelligence, the talent for creative inventiveness, and the astute intuitive perception that lies within folks who are common and who do not compete for results. These are folks who live ordinary average lives. For winners and losers alike, the challenge is to find the brilliance in the unspectacular—the breeding ground for all human brilliance.

The common threads of everyday living often involve struggle, suffering, and mundane moments. The content and context of these experiences give birth to the inner brilliance that exists in people from all walks of life. For example, the acclaimed physician created his brilliance during long arduous hours of training and preparation. Those with academic scholarship achieved brilliance through hours of study and preparation. Talented Olympic athletes are up early training regardless of weather. Boxers do their roadwork and run early when many are fast asleep. Working class folks sacrifice and do what needs to be done without pomp and circumstance. There is a certain ongoing "daily-ness" to cultivating brilliance that is developed in these mundane, unspectacular moments in life. These everyday struggles make heroes and heroines out of common ordinary people.

Kids and the Zero-Sum Perspective

Parents can create barriers for their children that make it difficult for the kids to embrace their inner brilliance. Unwittingly, parents can foster a win-at-all-costs mentality when their child participates in sports, academics, or other activities.

Danny Almonte, a Little League player, was the talk of the Bronx during the summer of 2001. With his high leg kick and a fastball that reached a top speed of 76 miles per hour (at Little League distance, that is the equivalent of a 103 mile per hour major league fastball), Danny became a summer sensation. His imposing frame won him the nickname of "Little Unit"—a reference to Randy "Big Unit" Johnson, a 6-foot, 10-inch major league baseball player at the time.

In 2001, Danny pitched a perfect game in the Little League World Series, the first since 1979, leading his team to a third-place finish in the series. His team was referred to as the "Baby Bombers" because they played in the shadows of Yankee Stadium. They quickly became the feel-good story of the 2001 Little League World Series. After the series, during a Yankees game, New York mayor Rudy Giuliani honored them with the key to the city.

Rumors, however, about Almonte's age swirled. It was quickly confirmed that he was two years too old to legally play Little League. His father, Felipe, falsified his records. ESPN labeled Felipe Almonte, "the worst stereotype of the Little League parent sprung to life."[4]

Some parents will do almost anything to get their "junior" in the spotlight. During my boyhood days of Little League, I never witnessed a fight between players while playing the game. However, I did observe three different fights between parents and my coach Bernie Nale. He was fair to the players and stubborn and cantankerous with parents who did not like how he played their kids. Parents and coaches can lose perspective about the purpose of Little League in a child's life. When Little League becomes more about the parents' lives and less about a child developing the capacity to play, the resulting environment makes it difficult for children to discover their inner brilliance.

Many parents attempt to fulfill their unlived lives through their children. In March 2019, the FBI uncovered a college admissions scandal where several parents used bribery and other forms of fraud to illegally arrange to have their children admitted to top colleges and universities. Several, including wealthy and celebrity

---

4. Jim Caple. "Nobody Wins When the Winners Cheated," ESPN.com, September 2, 2001.

families, faced felonies, fines, and jail sentences in their attempt to help their children win in life. I've witnessed attempts to control their child's academic future in Little League too.

When my kids played baseball, one couple got into a major argument with the coach for playing their kid in the wrong position. They argued that the coach was screwing up their son's opportunity for a college scholarship. The boy was just ten years old. The parents wanted to control their child's future by arguing with the coach. Certainly, during these times the view of inner brilliance dims. When parents direct unnecessary energy and sacrifice toward a child's sport or academic pursuits in an attempt to help their child achieve a desired goal, the child learns that power and influence over the coach is more important than cultivating their inner brilliance. What gets lost is helping the child make meaningfulness out of whatever position he is asked to play or be in.

According to Zendaya of the Disney sitcom *Shake It Up*, "*Shake It Up* definitely teaches kids about the importance of reaching for your dreams and setting high goals. It also teaches great lessons about friendship and family." In a psychological study of students who enrolled in four-year colleges, it was affirmed that goal-setting programs appear to be a quick, effective, and inexpensive intervention for struggling undergraduate students.[5] Yet, many of us as parents go over the top, attempting to set our children up for success no matter what. The intensity that a parent expends to pave the way for a child to succeed is often more harmful than helpful to the child's overall understanding of the meaning of life.

---

5. Dominique Morisano, Jacob B. Hirsh, Jordan B. Peterson, Robert O Pihl, and Bruce M. Shore. "Setting, Elaborating, and Reflecting on Personal Goals Improves Academic Performance," *Journal of Applied Psychology 95*, no. 1 (March 2010): 255–264.

A parent's insistence on excellent results often contributes to a kid's distorted view of performance results in life and obscures the awareness of the inner beauty of brilliance.

With team sports, the beauty of inner brilliance is uncovered in the everyday experience. Kids have fewer memories of the wins or losses and more about their relationships with team members. Conversations mostly occur about the interactions and behaviors they have had with others. Fond memories regarding the grind and discipline of training are wrapped around the stories of everyday experience. Team members recognize the brilliance of managing pressure and difficult times because they share the struggle with each other.

Us versus Them

Zero-sum mentality reduces life to winners and losers. Results amount to either success or failure. Winners are those who work hard enough and want to win bad enough. Losers are everybody else. When being a winner makes someone else a loser, life becomes "us" versus "them." It fuels a crab mentality, which is a kind of selfish, short-sighted thinking that concludes, "If I can't have it, neither can you."

We can absolutize the world into winners and losers; good guys and the bad guys—and we're always the good guys. With this perspective, it becomes easy to lose sight of our inner brilliance. Focusing on winning and losing becomes a barrier to understanding that each person is an unrepeatable miracle of the universe. Within each of us is this unknown creative energy identified as inner brilliance that is unpredictable and immeasurable.

Barrier #2—Being versus Doing

*To be nobody but yourself in a world which is doing its
best, night and day, to make you everybody else means to
fight the hardest battle which any human being can fight;
and never stop fighting.*

—E. E. CUMMINGS

Poet E. E. Cummings framed the battle to be yourself correctly. So much of life is about the pressure of others in the world attempting to squeeze you into a mold that is not the authentic you. The seduction is to lose yourself in doing what would please others at the price of losing your sense of being. It is a subtle, relentless compression that can crush the awareness of inner brilliance.

James Baldwin, the great African American playwright and essayist, wrote, "You know, it's not the world that was my oppressor, because what the world does to you, if the world does it to you long enough and effectively enough, you begin to do to yourself." Barriers to embracing brilliance in average spaces of life are often self-constructed through the dynamic that Baldwin described.

Our Children Are Watching

Our parents are, unwittingly, one of the great barriers toward uncovering brilliance in everyday places. We learn to focus on doing before we ever understand our precious sense of being. Psychotherapists such as the renowned John Bradshaw, Alice Miller, and Marilyn Murray have written that when parents do not spend necessary time with the child on their terms, essentially valuing their being, that the child will turn to achievement behaviors in an attempt to be important. It is the child's desperate attempt to know that they matter to the parent.

According to Bradshaw and Miller, this becomes a classic setup for a child to become a human doing versus a human being. Parents are responsible for so many thousands of hours of influence. Bradshaw contends that we can know that Mom and Dad love us by the way they provide basic needs such as shelter, food, clothing, and education. However, he states that we only know that we (our being) matters when Mom and Dad carve out special time to be with us on our terms and not theirs.

Children focus on what matters to parents and seek approval through achieving desired results in hopes of gaining the parents' needed attention and approval. According to Alice Miller, when Mom and Dad get so involved with work and outside activities at the expense of spending time with the children, kids subtly learn that who they are matters less than what they do. Children notice what matters to Mom and Dad and then pursue that to get the smile of approval and attention from their parents.

For example, the father of one my patients is a pastor who spends all his time in his ministry. My patient became a pastor too and spends all his time in his ministry, just like his father. His crisis is one of identity. If he wasn't a pastor, he'd lose his identity. Even when his father said, "Son, I love and accept you for who you are. Don't fear rejection from your mother and me if you leave the ministry," it resonated with a hollow ring for my patient. Throughout my patient's entire life, his father modeled to him that ministry was who he was. Now that he questions his desire to do professional ministry, a crisis erupts because his identity is tied into his profession. His life doing has blinded him to his precious being and has become a barrier to his inner brilliance.

Some children motivated by despair and discouragement that somehow getting parental attention is never going to happen do the opposite of their parents. It is common for children to rebel against this lack of attention. Many children become human doings because their essence of being was long abandoned.

Spending Time with Our Children in Spontaneous Ways

Children get set up to avoid their inner brilliance, which is fostered and developed in the average space of just being a child. Inner brilliance is cultivated when parents simply spend time with the child on their terms. For example, my father-in-law, Wendell, lived about an hour and a half from us in Arizona. When my boys were young, he would come and get each of them, one at a time, to spend special time with him at his home. I recall watching from a distance how he worked with my youngest son, Sam. When he was maybe four years old, Sam would take his grandpa by the finger and guide him all over the backyard and even into the neighbor's yard. If Sam wanted to climb a tree, that's what they did. If Sam wanted to dig a hole, that's what they did. I will never forget how Wendell totally dedicated his time to Sam during his special outing. He role modeled being available and present on Sam's terms.

In this way, a child learns that he is not only loved but that he matters. He learns that who he is and what he prefers to do or not do is important. This can only occur when parents step back and let their child *be* without judgment.

Author and psychological consultant Marilyn Murray's description of the Scindo Syndrome in her book *The Murray Method* underscores the importance of parents spending significant time with their children on their terms. Some parents may view this as not important. However, children feel valued and loved when they are allowed to play spontaneously under the caring watch of a parent who participates in the child's extemporaneous play. This kind of activity lets the child know he matters. When this occurs frequently, it fosters the soulfulness of a child and plants seeds of creativity in average mundane moments that cannot grow in any other environment. When this does not happen often, children adopt a false self that promotes doing what is expected for approval versus expressing a spontaneous being. The natural, free-spirited being is lost as they try to get the smile of approval from the parent, thus avoiding abandonment and neglect. Sadly, this loss occurs subconsciously to the child and parents are unaware of the consequences.

Children learn to believe that they don't matter from overt and blatant messages from their parents, but the transition is subtle. It most often happens when children conclude that if Mom and Dad are not spending time with them, it is because they don't matter. Children don't have the capacity to think that parents have their priorities out of balance. So, they internalize messages of mistaken belief, such as "I don't measure up," or "If I have to depend upon someone else to meet my needs it will never happen," or "My value is determined by my performance." Once internalized, these and other messages become a barrier to finding inner brilliance from average places of childhood development.

Barrier #3— A Rule-Breaker's Mentality

Sports teaches you character, it teaches you to play by the rules, it teaches you to know what it feels like to win and lose—it teaches you about life.

—BILLIE JEAN KING

When we lose our sense of being in all that we do, we become more vulnerable to living our lives with a zero-sum mentality, which breeds a rule-breaker's mentality. This mentality is an attitude that suggests that it is okay for me to break the rules because I am a special exception and the rules do not apply to me. This attitude of entitlement is pervasive throughout society. The world of sports is a glaring example. The combination of an over emphasis upon winning and the commercialization of sports fuels a grandiose and pompous environment that tarnishes the pure love for the sport and accelerates a distorted view of the sport itself.

There is a story about this subtle snag of grandiosity in *The Spirituality of Imperfection* by Ernest Kurtz and Katherine Ketchum: A past president of the Hazelden Foundation, a leading treatment resource for alcohol and drug addiction, was approached by a young researcher asking, "Why is it that even intelligent alcoholics can get so trapped in denial of their alcoholism? Is it because of grandiosity—they think that they can do anything to their bodies and survive, they think that they are 'too smart' to be alcoholic? Or is it because of self-loathing—they despise themselves and feel they deserve to die, if they are alcoholics?"

The past president sighed and replied, "The alcoholic's problem is not that he thinks he is very special. Nor is the alcoholic's problem that he thinks he is a worm. The alcoholic's problem is that he is convinced "I am a very special worm!"[6]

Likewise, sports can teach an athlete that "I am a very special worm." In an attempt to promote a child's brilliance through performance excellence, parents often lose sight of the beauty of inner brilliance that resides inside the heart of a child. This emphasis projects a drive to perform that often fuels a rule-breaking mentality. By emphasizing a "no matter what it takes" mentality, parents can cultivate a scarcity mentality of never having enough. This can accelerate grandiosity in a child that leads to a rule-breaking attitude that says, "I am a very special worm, so I can cross whatever boundaries I want." It becomes grotesque and ugly when carried into adulthood. There is always a serious price to pay when a parent chooses to emphasize outer excellence in performance over the cultivation of inner brilliance of spirit.

Parents can fuel this mentality through Little League and other organized sports for kids. Unfulfilled dreams of parents can become grandiose expectations for children, particularly when the child demonstrates special talent to throw or hit a baseball. Parents conclude that their child deserves special consideration in family or at school because of their talent. When the parent believes their child is being treated unfairly, then he or she raises hell with the coach. A common retaliation goes something like, "Either my son/daughter will play a certain amount or a certain position or we will pull him/her off the team and go play elsewhere."

All too often, if the child is good enough, concessions are made, and suddenly the child is awakened to the experience of

---

6. Earnest Kurtz and Katherine Ketchum. *The Spirituality of Imperfection: Storytelling and the Search for Meaning* (New York: Bantam, 1993), 189.

special privilege. He notices that he can demand what he wants and get it because he has special talent and learns that he is an exception to the rule. Sports is not the only contributing factor to this grandiose attitude, but it provides common fuel to this "special worm" mentality.

Then college recruiting begins with elaborate promises made to lure and treat the teenager. He or she is given celebrity status. "Special worm" treatment includes anything from incidental privileges to secret payments given to the athlete or family or both, depending on how good of an athlete they might be. It is big business with a strategy of farming big bucks for the university. This rule-breaking mentality is by now well ensconced in the understanding and awareness that an athlete brings into the next level of life.

Professional organizations escalate the rule-breaker's mentality. They fuel the challenge by giving athletes anything they want, as long as they continue to perform to a certain level of excellence. The mentality is do whatever you must to win a championship, including breaking the rules. So, you have cheating in every sport—bike racing with the infamous Lance Armstrong who was stripped of all seven Tour de France victories in 2012. In 2007, the McLaren Formula One race team was fined $100 million for cheating. In the same year, the New England Patriots were fined $750,000 for cheating and spying on other teams.

In baseball, there was an era of cheating when players engaged performance enhancing drugs. It became the steroid era in baseball. Between the early 1990s and mid-2000s, players hit an unprecedented number of home runs. Owners, players, and fans alike all conspired. Players loved the results steroids produced. Owners loved the revenue that came in. Fans loved the excitement of all the home runs and the celebrated home run race between Sammy Sosa and Mark McGuire in 1998. All concerned turned their eye to the rapidly increasing physical size of the players and how these amazing statistics were being compiled.

More was just better until José Canseco wrote his bombshell book: *Juiced: Wild Times, Rampant 'Roids, Smash Hits, and How Baseball Got Big* in February 2005. In this book he told on himself and a ton of others who broke the rules with steroid use. At first, most people wrote off his statements and accused Canseco of acting out sour grapes about baseball. But today the detractors are silent, and the offending players have become the scapegoat for the league and our society.

The rule-breaking mentality is role modeled in every profession at every level of society. Politicians, ministers, coaches, teachers, police officers, doctors, and lawyers (not to mention all kinds of addicts) have all been guilty of feeling entitled to break the rules. The impact on the worldwide community is astounding. Cheating always has devastating consequences. Perhaps, the most subtle but greatest is that those who learn to break the rules sacrifice the cultivation of inner brilliance.

Barrier #4— Egotism

"What's this?"

"A needle."

"What should I do with it?"

*"Please use it to pop your head.
It's obscuring my view of the room."[7]*

—ILONA ANDREWS, *MAGIC STRIKES*

7. Ilona Andrews. *Magic Strikes* (New York: Ace, 2009), 63.

Through my many years of treating addiction, I have learned that most addicts have allowed their egos to dominate and take up too much space. It's true before and after recovery. It's as if you were to blow up a huge balloon in a room that takes up all the space so that all the addict's friends and loved ones were smashed against the wall. An addict will take up all the air and space with ego. Even in recovery, the focus is on either keeping the addict sober or providing them with what they need. Through hypervigilance, we do whatever we have to do to not trigger the addict to act out. It becomes all about the addict so that no one else in the family matters like the addict does. This is a common concern that families of addicts share with me.

Some of my clients who are athletes would not give up their pursuit of championships even if it cost them their families. This idea that you are what you have or do comes from ego, and it distorts much of the everyday experience of the average life that we all share. With this distortion, ego prevents us from discovering our inner brilliance. Fame, attention, and possessions trigger drunken distortion about life values and intoxicate our importance. It is so difficult to take in the value of average daily living and find inner brilliance when a person is stuck in a prima donna lifestyle.

Ego can lead to short-sighted thinking and out-of-control behavior. It can block sensitivity to others and to our own behaviors. When my youngest son, Sam, was playing a game on a summer baseball league, his coach became annoyed about the umpire's calls. The tipping point came when the umpire made a controversial call that Sam's coach did not agree with. He ran out to the umpires to protest. The coach ramped up, and things got pretty heated. The coach just wouldn't back off after the umpire gave him plenty of opportunity.

After sufficient warning, the umpire threw the coach out of the game. Here's where things went awry: The coach stepped back, folded his arms across his chest, and expressed his ego: "No, I'm not leaving—you guys are leaving because I am firing you both!"

With that said, the umpires gathered their equipment and left. The coach appointed his assistant coaches to finish the game as umpires. He made a complete ass of himself in front of the kids and parents. After the game, he gathered the kids in the outfield to go over the usual debriefing. During the short talk, the coach made a few statements about players who played well and key mistakes but didn't say a single word about the umpires.

The coach missed a golden opportunity to cultivate the inner brilliance of humility. It would have been a teachable moment if the coach apologized to the kids and parents for his behavior toward the umpires. He could have demonstrated that even if you are the coach, it's not okay to act egotistical, but when you do, the sensible thing to do is to apologize. He could have shared that he would make amends to the umpires and pay them double for their embarrassment. Instead, he acted with his ego, and the kids walked away with the lesson that it is okay to break the rules and be a jerk to protect your ego if you're the one in charge.

Being Vulnerable Can Help Access Your Inner Brilliance

Inner brilliance is given birth and grows in a spirit of humility. Only when you are humble is it possible to be vulnerable when failure and brokenness happens. Another way of expressing vulnerability is becoming "emotionally naked" so that people can see you on the inside.

A lot of people are afraid to be seen on the inside because they think, *If you know what I know about me, you will reject me.* Some people shrink from the discovery of their own brilliance because they fear they will be judged as not good enough or simply average. Vulnerability risks being judged as weak. Many do not consider showing weakness as an act of courage. To share vulnerable feelings of tears and sadness is understood to emasculate a man, undermining his power in manhood.

This misperception of vulnerability discourages men from becoming emotionally naked to their partners, family, and friends. It creates distance from inner brilliance because of a fear of rejection. As a result, many live their lives in quiet desperation, to borrow a phrase from Thoreau. Many men have learned to avoid being vulnerable, citing that their parents never taught them how to express their feelings and that not to do so bids them well in society. To be vulnerable and emotionally needy is to be perceived as sniveling. The emphasis is on don't whine and complain.

The truth is, it demands great courage to be vulnerable, to expose and sit with the hurt and pain of human failure. Researcher and author Brené Brown suggests, "Vulnerability is the core, the heart, the center of meaningful human experiences."[8] Authors Ernest Kurtz and Katherine Ketcham add that human connection happens not on the basis of common strength, rather through shared weakness.[9] It is the shared honesty of mutual vulnerability openly acknowledged. Yet, many who are perceived as valiant and brave by society's standards are in truth dominated by the fear of

---

8. Brené Brown. *Daring Greatly: How the Courage to Be Vulnerable Transforms the Way We Live, Love, Parent, and Lead* (New York: Avery Publishing, 2012), 12.

9. Earnest Kurtz and Katherine Ketchum. *The Spirituality of Imperfection: Storytelling and the Search for Meaning* (New York: Bantam, 1993), 204.

further pain from moments of personal failure. Hiding vulnerability is perceived as protection.

When we embrace vulnerability, our inner brilliance can create the resilience needed to reboot, revive, and overcome defeat. Through inner brilliance, we transform the ashen taste of ordinary results and even abject failure into the meaningful fruit of purpose and perspective. Our brilliance creates the solution for healing and meaningful living and transforms outside behavior.

Questions

Take some time to create a conversation name tag on an index card. Divide your card into four sections. Answer the following questions and place each of your answers in one of the four sections of the card:

1. Can you think of a time when you were growing up where you experienced a parent or other adult pushing you or other kids to win when it seemed a little over the top? What might they have done differently to make things less intense?

2. How did you learn to emphasize "doing" over "being" in your childhood?

3. Who role modeled rule-breaking behavior in your life?

4. Can you think of an experience or time in your life where your behavior demonstrated an "I want what I want when I want it" mentality?

After writing down each response on your card, have a conversation with your partner or a friend about your experiences.

Chapter 4

Four Benefits of Embracing Average

Commonality with other people carries with it all the meanings of the word common. It means belonging to a society, having a public role, being part of that which is universal. It means having a feeling of familiarity, of being known, of communion. It means taking part in the customary, the commonplace, the ordinary, and the everyday. It also carries with it a feeling of smallness, or insignificance, a sense that one's own troubles are 'as a drop of rain in the sea.' The survivor who has achieved commonality with others can rest from her labors. Her recovery is accomplished; what remains before her is her life.

—JUDITH LEWIS HERMAN, *Trauma and Recovery: The Aftermath of Violence—From Domestic Abuse to Political Terror* enry Ward Beecher wrote, "The art of being happy lies in the power of extracting happiness from common things." In a thumbnail sketch, these authors share the value and benefit of the average and the commonplace. Commonality is so frequent and repetitious in all our lives that we must make something meaningful of it. There are four benefits for those of us who embrace the average, mundane, day-to-day living experience that connects us to our personal brilliance.

Benefit # 1—Personal Power through Telling Your Story

We tell ourselves stories in order to live.

—JOAN DIDION, writer and journalist,
The White Album

There is no greater agony than bearing an untold story inside you.

—MAYA ANGELOU, poet, memoirist,
and civil rights activist

Everyone has a story to tell. The magic of healing is contained within the context of storytelling. And the greatest stories come from average everyday living. For me, the single greatest tool for my personal healing has been my own story. There has been no greater healing source. Housed in every life story is the truth that liberates. This is why Alcoholics Anonymous (AA) has been so powerful for so many for so long. Within the community of alcoholics there are "shared stories." Each unique story is tied together through a shared weakness.

In *One Minute Wisdom*, Anthony de Mello writes, "The Master gave his teaching in parables and stories, which his disciples listened to with pleasure—and occasional frustration for they longed for something deeper. The Master was unmoved. To all their objections he would say, 'You have yet to understand, my dears, that the shortest distance between a human being and Truth is a story.' Another time he said, 'Do not despise the story. A lost gold coin is found by means of a penny candle; the deepest truth is found by means of a simple story.'"[10]

It has been my experience that all the therapeutic healing arts are dependent upon human story. The greatest healing truths can be uncovered only through unpacking the intricate details of one's story. Carl Jung concluded that every person has a story, and when derangement occurs, it is because the personal story has been denied or rejected. Healing and integration come when people discover or rediscover their personal story. Voicing our story is that important.

Social psychologist Aleks Krotoski, in her book *Untangling the Web*, proclaims that, "Stories are memory aids, instruction manuals and moral compasses."[11] In *The Secret Life of Bees*, Sue Monk Kidd states that, "Stories have to be told or they die, and when they die, we can't remember who we are or why we're here."[12]

No One Passes through Childhood into Adulthood Unscathed

Many people have experienced tragic stories of abuse. Because their experiences were so painful, they tend to avoid the direct

---

10. Anthony de Mello. *One Minute Wisdom* (New York: Doubleday, 1988).
11. Aleks Krotoski. *Untangling the Web.* (London: Faber & Faber, 2013).
12. Sue Monk Kidd. The Secret Life of Bees. (New York: Penguin Books, 2005).

impact of their story through a cocktail of strategies often including drugs, alcohol, and sex. The fear of what they'd feel if the immense pain resurfaced is motivation to elude facing the agony in their story.

It is not uncommon to hear someone declare, "I grew up in a perfectly happy childhood." Usually, this signals that someone is minimizing significant hurtful experiences. In some cases, upon deeper exploration, we learn that neglect and abandonment were normalized and marginalized. Likewise, while horrifying traumas can be obvious, minor trauma is often minimized and overlooked.

No one goes through childhood and avoids disappointment and other hurts. There are major traumas and minor traumas. All are significant. Frequently, people have learned to practice an unspoken rule in their family to "embrace the improbable and ignore the obvious." But make no mistake. Minor traumas affect us. There is a pool of pain that must be drained for personal healing to occur. That pool of pain encompasses the average everyday experiences of our childhood that were hurtful, whether major or minor. For many, unmet emotional needs were never addressed as they were invisible. Understanding the impact of these "minor" traumas in average everyday living takes focused effort.

Fritz Perls, credited as the father of Gestalt therapy, an existential/experiential form of psychotherapy that emphasizes personal responsibility and focuses on the individual's experience in the present moment, stated, "Nothing changes until it becomes what it is."[13] Most of us have learned to ignore the obvious and embrace the improbable in our life stories. We sort of walk "around the

---

13. Fritz Perls. *When is Enough, Enough?* (Center City, MN: Hazelden, 1997), 6.

dead dog" in the living room when it comes to our unmet emotional needs from ordinary past experiences.

The prosaic influence of the Catholic Church and the devastation of World War I had an obvious impact on the writings of J. R. R. Tolkien in the creation of *The Hobbit* and *The Lord of the Rings*. The commonplace drudgery of everyday living in African American communities of the South had an obvious impact on Maya Angelou in her poetry and other writings. Yet, most of us minimize the normal but painful experiences in our personal lives and embrace the improbable conclusion that these commonplace occurrences had little impact on who we are. Consequently, we learn to disdain the average experience. We learn to forget its meaningful impact as we surge to find the "ring" that will make discomfort immediately vanish.

It takes courage to tell our stories and deepen our awareness of what is real. We are often afraid to unravel the uneventful, uncomfortable times of our past. We fear that if we do unravel them, our notions of reality will disintegrate, and all that what we have always thought to be true will crumble into nothingness. Yet, personal healing demands that we tell our story to uncover the meaningfulness that exists when we allow ourselves to lean into the pain.

Philosopher and theologian Soren Kierkegaard wrote, "Life must be lived forward but can only be understood backward." Looking to the past for understanding is a priceless undertaking for those who want to make meaningfulness from what is commonplace and real. Story is about saying it straight. Say what you mean and mean what you say. Just don't say it with meanness. In a Twelve Step meeting, one person described ignoring his story was like "shoving a stick of dynamite up my ass and thinking I was going to outrun it."

The Brilliance Found in the Average Story

Every childhood tells a story that if listened to will crack the shell of brilliance that exists within. I was born and raised in a little town called Mattoon in east central Illinois. As a small child, I grew up in a large two-story house on Seventeenth Street. I had eight brothers and sisters, and I was the youngest boy. My parents raised my oldest sister's three children in addition to their own. There was constant tension and chaos throughout my childhood. There was much reason for anxiety, insecurity, and uncertainty. As a young child, I remember different experiences that triggered me to embrace the improbable and ignore the obvious.

I had a very active imagination. I used it to navigate my way through boredom, loneliness, and fear. I remember going to bed on a summer's night. At the time, my bedroom faced Mr. and Mrs. Hill's house next door to the north. From my bed, the box fan would be on in one of two windows that were side by side. The hum of the fan blocked out all other noise. On some nights, the fan helped me drift off to sleep.

On other nights while lying in bed, I would look out the window, past the Hill's backyard, and view the weeping willow tree in Mr. Selby's backyard at the corner of our block. A huge tree limb had been sawed off at an angle. It had broken and needed to be cut away and Mr. Selby could only reach it by sawing it off at an angle.

On this particular late summer's night, with a constant steady breeze blowing the leaves and branches of that willow tree back and forth—combined with the fear of the dark in a young boy's imagination—the weeping willow tree transformed into an evil demon with a long flowing beard who had a sword. I was sure he was going to slit my throat just as soon as I dropped off to sleep. I recall fighting off sleep desperately to save my life. I would count as high as I could. I would try to count the stars in the sky. I would do anything, everything to fight off the inevitable doom. Yet, despite all of my heroic efforts, I would succumb to the unconsciousness of a deep sleep. When I woke up the next morning, I looked out at that tree and once again saw a friendly weeping willow. But the next night, the evil demon was back!

I have thought about that weeping willow tree many times throughout my adult years. After being an addict in recovery for thirty years, I am still haunted with fear triggered by an active imagination. I can get stuck in the mental wool of believing nothing is ever going to work out. It's like trying to run away from a monster in a dream that I can't get away from. I can feel paralyzed by my addiction and think I have no choice but to comply with the dictates and urges of addictive cravings. Fear can trigger my mind into a spin cycle of a victim mentality, where I conclude that I am screwed no matter what I do.

During these times, I drag myself to a meeting and connect with real people who live just like me. In the safe confines of that meeting, it is as if the sun comes up and I can see the light of hope. All the fear melts away, and the cravings disappear. Then I tell myself—*What's wrong with you? This is the real world!* But when I leave the safe cocoon of community, the addictive cravings descend upon me and just like the evil demon at night in the willow tree, the monster of addiction comes back! And so it is, until I leave the meeting—and then the monster comes back!

When I was that young boy, I found a way to solve my dilemma with the willow tree. I simply moved into the bedroom on the other side of the house. Rather than being tantalized with the fear of the tree monster, I was able to look into the Nale family's backyard on the south side of our house, where there was a basketball court. At that time, I just loved basketball. I recall falling asleep dreaming about draining a buzzer beater and playing in the NBA. My solution was a win/win. There was no monster wielding a sword nearby, and I got a good night's sleep.

Sometimes, simple choices for change go a long way to make a big difference. There are times when simple choices are the best for managing addictive urges. Rather than sit and stew, wrestling with urge, the simple solution was to go to a Twelve Step meeting and share my story of craving. I deescalated the urge simply by talking about it. I transformed the monster of addiction by telling the story of my urges—my average everyday experiences of life.

Through these many years, I have probably shared my life story more than fifteen hundred times and counting. I explore themes such as shame, deprivation, and a host of other important motifs. I share how I convert the average and commonplace into brilliant insight and wisdom toward positive competence and capability that creates lifelong change.

The value of excavating and sharing story in detail can be overlooked. I have discovered the power of wisdom uncovered through sifting and sorting life story with a fine-tooth comb. Inevitably, the greatest recovery brilliance is housed within the context of every person's life story. It is a gold mine ready to be unearthed for those who are willing to do the work of discovery.

Benefit #2—You Create Authentic, Intimate Connections with Self and Others

Real intimacy is a sacred experience. It never
exposes its secret trust and belonging to the
voyeuristic eye of a neon culture. Real intimacy is
of the soul, and the soul is reserved.[14]

—JOHN O'DONOHUE,
Anam Cara: A Book of Celtic Wisdom

I hate solitude, but I'm afraid of intimacy.
The substance of my life is a private conversation
with myself which to turn into a dialogue would be
equivalent to self-destruction. The company which I
need is the company which a pub or a cafe will provide.
I have never wanted a communion of souls. It's
already hard enough to tell the truth to oneself.[15]

—IRIS MURDOCH, *Under the Net*

Being honest with myself at the deepest level has always been the most difficult task I have ever known. Yet without this honesty, the depth of meaningfulness in life is blunted. Average experiences remain just that—average, with no depth of insight.

Without honesty there is no authenticity. Without authenticity, average everyday experience fails to have impactful meaning. We live life unchallenged and boredom eats away at us. Dishonesty becomes a way of embracing the improbable and ignoring what is obvious. It makes average experience empty of brilliance and drains creative resources.

---

14. John O'Donohue. *Anam Cara: A Book of Celtic Wisdom* (New York: Harper Perennial, 1996), 17.

15. Iris Murdoch. *Under the Net* (New York: Penguin Books, 1982), 61.

Brilliance is unleashed in the depths of honesty. Yet, there is a great price. To become emotionally naked to oneself is courageous. To open your heart with that same honesty to another person is at best a risky encounter.

Getting Emotionally Naked

Getting emotionally naked with reality is a scary proposition. Facing personal brokenness risks tearing away the fabric and sometimes even the foundation of meaning for your life. Ripping away the facade of delusional thinking can feel terrifying—like free falling with no bottom.

In 1989, I was forced to get emotionally naked in a very dramatic way. I was serving on the pastoral staff of a church in Denver. I had worked at the church for thirteen years and then left to pastor a church in Kansas City. After two years of ministry in Kansas City, I abruptly left the church to return to the Denver church. The senior pastor of the Denver church had hired an assistant to cover the responsibilities that I once did. However, the assistant did not work out well and left. The senior pastor wanted me to come back to cover my old position. His lure was promising me he would do everything he could to ensure I would take over the Denver church when he retired.

What I did not know when I accepted this offer was that the senior pastor of the Denver church had used up all of his credits with the congregation. By that, I mean he had committed one too many errors and was being pressured to leave. This left me in a lurch. What would I do now? I had just moved my family to Denver from Kansas City. Would I be without a job? When he announced he had accepted a new job in Florida, he asked me to go with him with the same promise that he would have me become his executive pastor once he retired. It all happened so quickly, and I agreed to accept the position and planned to move to Florida in a few months. Yet, I believe divine providence had another idea.

At the church, I had become a veteran to crises. In my ministry I dealt with crises every week and sometimes daily. While at the Denver church, within a span of five years, I officiated funerals for ten different suicide victims. One even shot himself while I was attempting to get him to calm down over the phone. I was with his widow when she went to the morgue to identify his body. I will never forget the scream echoing down the concrete corridor that day when they pulled the curtain back for her to identify her husband's body. The face of the corpse had a look of horror, and her face was white ashen.

In early February 1989, I learned that one of the girls in my college ministry had just committed suicide. I recall going to the hospital with one of my colleagues. It was the same trauma hospital that I had been to so many times before. I walked into the family room and there were about ten to fifteen family and friends of the deceased. The father approached me and with a threatening voice said I was the reason why his daughter killed herself. In some strange way he thought it was my responsibility to prevent her from being released from a treatment center she was in. She left on her own, signed out, and went to her brother's apartment—the same brother who had previously molested her.

It wasn't the first time I had to deal with a crisis. Nor was it the first time I had been falsely accused. But, this time something snapped inside of me. Everything seemed to shift into slow motion. I don't remember responding to the accusation. I only remember walking away from the hospital and telling my colleague that something was not right. I began to unravel inside. I did not know what was going on. That night, I did not sleep. I couldn't get the girl's face out of my head. I was in a funk. Over the next few days, I walked around in a daze.

I stopped eating and over the next six weeks lost forty-eight pounds. I was decompensating and suffering from a major clinical depression. It was a free fall from reality and stability. I could not function. The suicide was a trigger, but I had more than fourteen years of intense workaholism under my belt. And it was slowly eating away at the core of my inner constitution.

Somewhere in all of that mix was the buildup of frozen, unresolved childhood trauma. During this time, the trauma reality began to thaw. Flashbacks of past hell streaked through my consciousness. It was a relentless Rolodex of tormented memories. I can't remember ever experiencing such intense pain, emotionally or physically, in all my days.

I began driving, alone and aimlessly, throughout the day and night. My head felt like an old washing machine, constantly churning back and forth. One day, a memory of me crossing sexual boundaries with one of my sisters surfaced. Different memories had been rolling around in my head about abuses perpetrated toward me. Now, I was confronted with my own acts of perpetration. At that point, it was too much. I felt as if I had fallen into an abyss. It was a bottomless free fall. I didn't want to live anymore.

I have heard others remark that suicide is the most selfish thing anyone could ever do. But at the time, for me, it seemed beyond choice. All I wanted was for the pain to stop. I was disconnected from everything except that one focus.

This next incident took place before the days of 9/11 and the enhanced security checkpoints, when anyone could go to a major airport and stroll through the concourses without check. One day, I decided to walk down a concourse and out one of the exit doors onto the runway and into the path of a jet taking flight. It never happened. Two dear friends had come looking for me. They found me and foiled my plan. In retrospect, I am forever grateful. To this day, these folks are the best friends I have ever known.

I was alive, but I spiraled downward for a long time. Things did not get better. I had tremendous anger inside about what I had done and what had been done to me. I drove around with all this rage inside. Once I travelled to an area of Denver called Five Points. Enraged and self-destructive, I tried to run down what I believed to be a gang of Crips. I did not know for sure if they were, but I thought if I antagonized them enough, they would surely shoot me. So I ran at them with my car and the gang dispersed pointing their fingers at me. I waited for sounds of gunfire but none came my way. Clearly, I was out of control.

My wife was scared for me and so was I. At the time, we had three young boys. I was unable to consider their needs. The thoughts and urges toward self-destruction were overwhelming. The emotional pain was more than I could handle. It felt as if I were falling into a bottomless pit, and I was unable to stop it.

I remember feeling totally detached from everything and everyone. I got to a point where without doubt, death was better than the pain inside. Finally, my wife and two friends convinced me to reach out for help. I was admitted to the psychiatric hospital in Columbine. I was there for three weeks.

The first night I stared at a piece of fuzz on the window for several hours. The attending nurse observed me doing it and did not say anything to me. I don't remember a lot about the interventions. I recall confronting and almost getting into a fight with another patient. We were watching television and he suddenly got up and threw his chair into the TV screen, destroying it. I got up to smack him, but five nurses intervened. Almost anything triggered my rage. I recall having this attitude that it didn't matter because I was convinced I was going to die anyway. This attitude melted away so much fear. I truly just didn't care anymore.

The hospital staff allowed me to spend time in the exercise room. I would beat the punching bag until every stitch of clothing was drenched in sweat, and I was totally exhausted. It felt good. So, they let me do it multiple times a day.

Once, during a particular rough patch, I found myself in the proverbial padded cell. The ceiling, walls, and floors were all padded. I remember thinking that my life and career were over. I had my Bible with me, and I opened it to Psalm 91. I read the verse out loud: "He who dwells in the shelter of the most high will rest in the shadow of the Almighty."

I thought about all the crap that my family and I had gone through in the church, and a wave of rage came over me. There were memories of a lot of sexual abuse. I felt the shame that manacled me and all of my siblings. I thought of the complexity of everything I knew about the church and its abuse. I wanted to throw up, but I did not. Rather, I began hitting my Bible with my bare fists. I struck my Bible again and again until my knuckles were bleeding. When I finished, I was totally exhausted. Not from the physical act of hitting but from tapping into all the rage, hate, and shame that had enveloped my life like a wet blanket for so many years.

My mind began to clear just a little. I recall being aware that if I could beat the hell out of my Bible and God still loved me, then I could live. In retrospect, I don't think I really cared whether God loved me. There have been many days that I certainly have not loved God. However, on that day, I chose to believe that I did love God. It provided relief in the moment.

The next day I committed to my wife that whatever it took, no matter how hard it may be, I was going to "hock my socks" if need be to get better. Slowly, I did. Over the following thirty years, I learned to manage depression. It has never left, and I deal with it to this very day. So I have learned to make depression a friend that helps me to be aware of my limitations. When I ignore my boundaries, physically or emotionally, depression reminds me and tells me something is out of balance. It is stubborn and powerful. If I do not pay attention, it will kick my ass.

In the beginning, Prozac and Xanax were helpful. I weened myself from Xanax and eventually was taken off Prozac. I would never have signed up for depression, but it has been a constant teacher. I lose my way when I try to do more than I can accomplish or try to be there for others without setting boundaries. However, when I accept boundaries and limits around my physical and emotional capabilities, I can become a resource for healing. It has helped me to cultivate a deeper spirituality. From tragic experience, I have carved out brilliant insight. Addressing heartbreaking experiences is a common thread that shows up through common shared brokenness. By leaning into it, we access our inner brilliance.

Benefit #3—Teaches the Fundamentals of Basic Self-Care in the Presence of Human Struggle

Struggle is the food from which change is made,
and the best time to make the most of a struggle is
when it's right in front of your face

—DANNY DREYER

DARE TO BE AVERAGE

If you stop struggling then you stop life.
—HUEY NEWTON

Every day, life is a struggle for someone, somewhere. Most often we struggle to avoid failure. The average entrepreneur suffers three to eight failures before experiencing success. It is inspirational when we hear the story of someone who has failed repeatedly only to eventually succeed. Yet, if we are honest about it, most people do not experience living happily ever after. Much of the world lives in squalor and poverty. Many are victimized with injustice. Millions of people experience far less privilege than the few who have accumulated material wealth. Yet the common thread that connects all of us together is the experience of struggle. Tragedy, death, loss, emotional, and physical pain are common bedfellows regardless of where or how we live.

Sadness and loss is the kind of struggle that can create a universal connection. I live in Arizona, where there are many inspirational and sad stories to tell about migrants crossing the mountainous desert in the southern portions of our state. One in particular is about a little girl traveling with her younger brother and uncle. They were being led through the mountainous terrain by a coyote—someone who is paid money to take people desperate to leave intolerable circumstances in their native land into the United States and, hopefully, into safety. When the migrants enter the United States, they are considered undocumented.

Usually, the coyote travels with a small contingency so as to not be noticed. In this case, the two children became exhausted and struggled to keep up with the pace set by the coyote. The disheartened uncle reached a point where he had to make a decision. He chose to carry the younger boy and allowed the older girl to struggle on her own. She quickly became disconnected from the traveling entourage and wandered lost in the desert. Eventually, she stumbled and fell. At some point, she died in the desert—cold, terrified, and all alone.

Deaths of this nature happen frequently in the vast mountainous Arizona desert. Most often, their bodies disappear, torn apart and eaten by desert wildlife. In this case, a humanitarian volunteer came upon her body. It took some time to determine what her name was and to notify her family. During the ensuing days, her travel story unfolded. She was traveling from Central America, seeking safety from violence. There was a grieving ceremony for her at the site where she died. In silence, those present were asked to contemplate her last moments alive on this earth. Those who gathered connected with her spirit, suffering the helpless despair she must have known during her final hours. Those present connected to the shared grief while focusing on the life and struggle of this endeared little girl.

In this tragedy, there were several questions that begged to be answered. Why did this have to happen? Can't there be another way of offering safety and support to vulnerable, innocent people? What about those in the desert who are never found? These questions lead to feelings of despair and anguish most of us attempt to avoid. They are common struggles that bypass the angst of what it would be like if it were your daughter or loved one who suffered this tragic ending. This is the part of life struggle that most people try to escape thinking about. We detach through the mind-numbing busyness of life. Yet, these losses through tragedy are far too common to ignore.

We all have limits on how much we are able to focus on the suffering in the world. Nevertheless, hellish and horrible tragedy is where the brilliance of human spirit is found. By emotionally connecting with the painful suffering of others, we create the brilliance of compassion—toward self and others.

Mother Teresa said, "Let us touch the dying, the poor, the lonely and the unwanted according to the graces we have received and let us not be ashamed or slow to do the humble work." Somehow, doing the humble work of connecting with the human spirit of a lost little girl in the desert offered powerful consolation in a moment of great anguish for many.

Buddhist monk and author Pema Chodron stated, "Compassion is not a relationship between the healer and the wounded. It's a relationship between equals." Only when we know our own darkness well can we be present with the darkness of others. Compassion becomes real when we recognize our shared humanity. Comfort and consolation is discovered when we connect with others who share the same common experience of suffering. To compartmentalize these thoughts to those who do the work of compassion professionally, social workers or clergy, would be to miss the opportunity to farm brilliance from an unwanted but common moments of struggle that we all share.

Strength and inspiration come in average moments when we share and connect with the human spirit of others. There is genuine depth in soothing a broken heart when we learn to stay in the presence of overwhelming discomfort. The human spirit is resilient and has the capacity to transform agony into poise and healing peace when discomfort and heartache is embraced and shared.

Benefit #4—Teaches the Difference between Being a Scoreboard and a Heart Champion

There's always the motivation of wanting to win. Every-body has that. But a champion needs, in his attitude, a motivation above and beyond winning.

—PAT RILEY

In our culture, we have an obsession with winning all the time. It is almost as if we suffer a kind of post traumatic stress disorder if judged as average. Our society places scoreboard champions on a pedestal. Winning is the pinnacle of meaning in life. Winning is everything. Anything short of winning is disdained and to be forgotten. Yet, as life unfolds, a common experience is that we learn more from our mistakes, failures, and losses than our successes and achievements.

There is no boundary to what a champion is driven to do to be number one. In the world of sport, unbelievable stories are told about players who compete with broken bones, damaged bodies, and mangled mental conditions—all for the sake of being lionized. The inference suggests that real champions ignore human limitations. That's what makes them champions.

In truth, scoreboard champions learn to depend on this kind of adrenaline to perform. It's no wonder the line gets blurred around performance enhancement drugs when champions are so monomaniacal about winning and avoiding losing. Being number one becomes an identity. As a result, life becomes imbalanced. Other aspects of life are often neglected. Relationships, spirituality, community values, and sensitivity to anything other than personal ambition suffer.

Addiction Becomes the Centerpiece

There are many whose performance is stellar and outstanding on the scoreboard of their professional life. Yet, the disparity of behavior away from their performance at work sabotages their life with addiction, which becomes the centerpiece. Trained to be champions in their field of endeavor, they know a lot about success but very little about the value of everyday living.

Scoreboard champions can evolve into addicts who become like little kids who cannot get enough sugar. You never get enough of what you really don't want. Eventually, in a downward death spiral, addiction gets lost in the delusional pursuit of one more hit, one more time that never ends.

In the beginning, you just want success, however it is defined. But in the end, the scoreboard mentality overwhelms and rather than you chasing the brass ring, the tables are turned and it begins to chase you. Like a pack of wolves chasing someone through the woods that keeps nipping at the heels, the addict keeps trying to reach for that hit one more time, while trying to keep the pack of wolves at bay. The thinking is: "I'm so close—yet so far away. I want to climb the hill just one more time." It's never sustainable. It only lasts but for a brief fleeting moment. Many scoreboard champions who come to see me as a therapist are left with the wreck and ruin of addiction's devastation.

Heart Champions

Heart champions are a different breed and are spawned from a different ilk. There is so much more than the score at the end of the game. Self-definition comes from a deeper source. It's about the preparation, the sacrifice, the sweat and engagement of uncertainty.

A heart champion's life is determined within—before the game is ever played and independent of the score at the end of the game. It has to do with connecting congruency with values of the heart. A heart champion is more concerned about being true to one's heart and not just winning or losing. Becoming true to your heart takes a willingness to go deeper and find meaningfulness in all of life's endeavors, including failure.

It's not like heart champions condition themselves to lose. Rather, they are carved from a deeper place down deep inside. A heart champion knows that losing is a part of the ebb and flow of life. She determines to never let an outcome define who she is. Instead, definition is determined by the vision of destiny from within which supersedes any result. Her priority is knowing that she is connected to herself, embracing all of herself—the good, the bad, and the ugly. She understands that life is a tapestry weaving together the bitter and the sweet, success and failure, triumph and tragedy. Positive results are fine and desired, but fundamentally, a heart champion already has determined that they are "an unrepeatable miracle of the universe." Heart champions understand that no victory will add to this reality and no defeat will take away from it. It is already etched into the stone of destiny that exists in their heart.

When Hall of Famers Embrace the Average

Baseball great Mickey Mantle once reflected on the average experience of his Hall of Fame baseball career. He said, "During my 18 years of major league baseball I came to bat almost 10,000 times.

I struck out about 1,700 times and walked another 1,800 times. You figure a ball player will have about 500 at bats a season. That means I played seven years without ever hitting the ball."[16]

The average experience of a baseball player is making an out, not getting a hit. In the presence of striving for success, even for someone as great as Mickey Mantle, there is a compelling story of difficulty and strife to share. Mantle's authentic willingness to connect with his intimate battle with failure forced him to practice fundamental basics of self-care. As a result, these commonplace experiences of struggle enabled him to look back at his Hall of Fame career and understand a difference between a scoreboard champion and a heart champion.

No matter who you are, transforming meaningfulness from mundane moments of struggle and failure is necessary to embrace the benefits of average commonplace struggles.

Questions

1. What parts of your life story have you never told yourself, let alone anyone else? Reflect on that part of your life story. What can you learn about yourself as you live life in a forward direction? Share your answers with a dear friend.

2. Getting emotionally naked with reality is a scary proposition. What part of your private reality do you struggle to face and share with anyone else?

---

16. Larry Canale. *Mickey Mantle—Memories and Memorabilia* (Iola, WI: Krause Publications, 2011), 150.

3. Think of a tragic event that you have experienced personally or have known others to endure. What ways have you learned to self-soothe in the presence of tragic loss?

4. In what ways has the concept of being a heart champion impacted your perspective of being a champion on the scoreboard (the outer results of success) in your life? Share with someone close to you who will listen.

Chapter 5

How to Begin—
Five Keys to Building
Your Community

The virtuous soul that is alone is like a lone burning coal;
it will grow colder rather than hotter.

—St. John of the Cross

Connection through community allows us to find meaningfulness in the average spaces in life. Millions in our world live disconnected from community. Without community, the likelihood of discovering our personal brilliance dims. Translating the ordinary into meaningfulness requires curiosity. This curiosity matures and grows best if we're in a community with others. Without it, we can become like a pinball between bumpers, reacting to what is around us and missing the journey inward that leads to brilliance. Connection in a safe community is key and crucial.

Several years ago, a woman lost a son in a single vehicle accident on his way to work. Her son had inspired many to live and dream big, face fears, and appreciate nature. He loved the outdoors and planned to one day live in his favorite state, Colorado, and become a teacher.

Some years after his death, the mom was visiting her oldest son who lived in Colorado Springs. She brought a picture of her deceased son with her on the trip. While there, she visited the Garden of the Gods with the beautiful towering sandstone formations. During her hike through the garden, she met a young man who was climbing, and she told him the story of her beloved deceased son. She asked if the climber would be willing to take her son's picture and wedge it under the highest rock that he scaled.

The young man respectfully suggested he take the picture with him and snap a photo of her son with him and his friends as they scaled each peak in Colorado. Each time after taking a photo, they would send it to her. Humbled by the gesture, this mother instantly felt connected to this young man she just met. Moments earlier, he was an isolated stranger. Now he was someone who helped her deeply connect to her lost loved one.

In an ordinary moment of grief and through the brilliance of two strangers, a beautiful moment of healing was created. This is how it is with community. We discover and cultivate connection, which brings us deeper into our heart, where the brilliance of healing lies.

Mother Teresa said, "Being unwanted, unloved, uncared for, forgotten by everybody, I think that is a much greater hunger, a much greater poverty than the person who has nothing to eat."

Do you know someone you would describe as forgotten? When you drive to work, worship, or play—do you notice the street people in your community? Not knowing what to do with misfortune, many look away from the homeless, choosing to deal with discomfort by distancing themselves from it. What about the person at the grocery store who shuffles by with a blank stare on his face? Do you think of him as invisible?

Folks warehoused in nursing homes across our country feel disenfranchised and forgotten. At this level of living, it really doesn't matter what possessions you once owned, who you have known, or really anything else. Being unloved, uncared for, and forgotten is the greatest poverty among the living. A fragmented, disenfranchised world distorts and undermines our potential for cultivating our brilliance in everyday places of living. Whether we realize it, we are communal creatures who need connection to understand the meaning of living. Isolation deadens connection like a cell phone when it's out of range. Community and commonality are important ingredients when fostering individual brilliance.

A safe and trusting community breeds safe emotional and physical touch. Here, vulnerability and trust is serendipitously expressed through our grief, joy, and challenge. I don't know anyone who exemplifies this truth more than my client, Sally.

Sally had every reason to isolate and avoid community when she first came to see me in my office. Emotionally, she was fragmented. She suffered horrendous physical, ritual, and sexual abuse from her parents who were involved in a cult. Her parents solicited her to other members of the family and cult. She experienced everything that would make a family unsafe. She fled from this frightful gruesome family to a life on the streets.

While learning plenty of street savvy, she also learned to stuff her sorrows and the sadism she'd experienced throughout her childhood with a cocktail of addictions. When she initially sought professional counsel, she experienced more abuse and betrayal from those who were supposed to be healing and safe. She learned to deaden herself to the world at large and to disconnect from community. Eventually, she decided to attend our intensive outpatient program, which involves sixty-five hours of therapy in eight days.

When she began her plunge experience, there was no trust, only desperation. However, as the days unfolded, her barriers began to come down. Maybe it was the intensity of one session after another beginning at 7:00 a.m. and continuing until 8:30 p.m. It could have been the many different approaches that her relentless counselors used. Whatever it was, she reached a watershed point where she made a decision to open her heart to the possibility of healing. As she progressed throughout the week, she made the decision that this would be her last attempt to find hope. She decided that she would do whatever it took to get healthy.

As she became committed to healing herself, she committed to integrating her fragmented inner self. She embraced the emotional pain that dominated her life, rather than medicate it with addiction. She resolved to attend Twelve Step meetings to address her compulsive behaviors. Though dominated with fear and full of anxiety, slowly she shifted and allowed her Twelve Step community to become a touchstone and signpost for reality in her recovery. Sharing her brokenness in community provided relational safety for Sally.

When there is relational safety in community, anything and everything can be explored and sifted and sorted through. Pain becomes the fellowship's touchstone and signpost indicating imbalance in life. Community provides a sound studio to listen to pain's message. Common shared brokenness is its draw, not common likeness or interest. Becoming emotionally naked by sharing our deepest feelings and secrets is commonplace and expected. It's a space where we can fit and be accepted as we are. It is a sanctuary in which to learn how we can wear our own skin well. It's a space to accept our own acceptance while staring at imperfection. It is a place to grow ourselves into adult maturity and discover inner brilliance.

Today, after many years of recovery and therapy, Sally has carved out a commitment to a Twelve Step community based on a shared brokenness that has proven supportive and sustaining. Today, though she continues to work out her emotional brokenness, she has become an inspiration to those who work with her professionally. She has become a leader in her field of expertise. Her husband and children continue to benefit from her resilience and commitment to her healing journey.

Recently, she told me her recovery life has rendered her 1,000 percent improved. She echoed that without a community to share her deepest feelings of brokenness, in concert with therapeutic intervention, her road to recovery would have led to a dead end.

I have led approximately 200 intense weekend workshops with men who are in recovery from sex addiction. Each session numbers about fifteen men, each involved in different groups, who have seriously committed to stop acting out. Most have been successful in doing so. Still, these men seek to emotionally grow themselves so that they experience more than sobriety. Their hope is to repair broken relationships and cultivate healthy relational intimacy with themselves and their committed partner.

These weekends have become a cocoon, a safe space to expose ugly intent, immature response, and emotional adolescence. Providing a container to express overwhelming sadness (usually via anger) with total acceptance is usually transformative and life changing for these men. Creating a space for someone to be livid and angry at another person who is present in respectful ways has been immensely helpful, even when they wanted to physically fight each other.

During one workshop, one guy told a story about something that happened at work. Another guy accused him of not acting like a man. Both men stared and postured, suggesting they were ready to clobber each other. Once the machoism and bluster settled, each realized that they would likely need to leave if they came to blows. Or they could kiss and make up. Thank God they chose the latter. Before the weekend was over, both learned to accept each other's differences, actually becoming closer because of the way they handled the altercation.

We create community to connect. It involves the courageous choice to be real and vulnerable. Within the context of groups, I have experienced men sharing their deepest pain with blood curdling cries of remorse, loss, and loneliness. Group therapy that becomes community is based on the mutuality of common shared brokenness. When people compete and compare themselves to others who have shared, the mutuality evaporates and group effectiveness no longer exists.

The famous testimony from Alcoholics Anonymous cofounder Bill Wilson—who was describing the night he paced back and forth in a lobby of a hotel in Akron, Ohio, craving for a drink—emphasized the power of mutuality. He said the impulse to drink was pushed out of his mind with the idea that "No, I don't need a drink—I need another alcoholic." This thought soon led him to connecting with Dr. Bob Smith, another alcoholic. Wilson later stated, "I knew I needed this alcoholic as much as he needed me."[17] This need for mutuality comes from common shared flaws and weakness. It creates a powerful oneness. This power is nurtured in a group through community spirit.

In community, there is shared vision, shared goals, and shared hope. There is healing power when a member courageously shares a truth he has not told to another living soul and then, in exchange, receives total love and acceptance from the group. There is healing when a member chooses to live in accountability and consultation with other group members. There is empowerment in a group when a group member, speaking from experience, confronts another member who is struggling to face the truth about his behavior. This makes the group powerful like no other.

The community becomes a safe space to confront ugly narcissism and grief and loss. It is a place built upon cooperation, not comparison and competition. It isn't the common strengths but the shared weaknesses that heal and promote personal brilliance. In the context of shared weakness, men have set aside their judgment and anger toward a brother's behavior and have extended compassion, identification, and care. The connection through the

---

17. Bill W., *Alcoholics Anonymous* (New York: Works Publishing Company, 1939), 1–16.

common bond of brokenness cultivates excitement and rejoicing rather than threat. Shared weakness is the cornerstone of true community.

The most powerful healing is the exploration of our story. Healing always leads to dependence upon our personal brilliance. Community is a place to define our limits and sharpen much-needed perspective regarding sobriety, serenity, and overall life balance. It is the training ground for the practice of living in consultation. Community curates personal brilliance by holding people accountable to their inner wisdom.

Some powerful collective wisdom has come from community consultation. This wisdom is sometimes passed from group to group via slogans. Some slogans about repeated destructive behaviors include: "If eight people tell you that you have a tail, the least you would do is look at your ass in the mirror"; "If you hang around the barbershop long enough, you're gonna get a haircut"; and "Is it working for you?" Simple. But powerful.

For me, the community of a men's group has become a resource for finding my lost voice. It is a place where I can sleuth the difference between aggression and assertion, victim and victimizer, and dependence and vulnerable interdependence in relationships. Finding our voice in community unlocks the door to going deep within one's reserve of brilliance and becoming one's own guru rather than looking for one outside of self. Grace Lee Boggs said it right when she wrote, "We are the leaders we have been looking and waiting for."[18]

---

18. Grace Lee Boggs. "We are the leaders we've been waiting for," *YouTube.com*, June 29, 2007, https://www.youtube.com/watch?v=DzeezIsTZ_o.

Community supports us when we are needy. It requires that we ask for what we need and face the fear of possible rejection and abandonment. These are the everyday common threads that connect us all and house the possibility of giving birth to personal brilliance. There is no greater space to cultivate and realize personal brilliance than in the context of healthy community. Community is the container that keeps us accountable to doing the work of carving consistency from everyday challenges that lead us to our brilliance.

Often, I hear someone complain that the group is not helpful and they get nothing from the group. Others say they attended ninety meetings in ninety days and still relapsed. While there is no guarantee that attending meetings will end relapse, there is a distinct approach to engaging community that can increase your odds or, at a minimum, make a profound difference in your life. I've summed them up in five points, and I offer them to you for consideration.

Key #1—Create and Maintain a Beginner's Mind-Set

George Eliot said, "It seems to me we can never give up longing and wishing while we are still alive. There are certain things we feel to be beautiful and good, and we must hunger for them." Yet hunger for being a beginner in spirit and attitude is a constant challenge for most of us. Most boxers, for example, lose focus after winning championships, in part because they stop being hungry and no longer embrace a beginner's mind-set. In growth and recovery, cultivating a beginner's mind-set is difficult. The space and place we do this is the terrain of everyday living, while addressing common uncomfortable feelings.

Almost every Twelve Step attendee can remember the first day he or she walked across the threshold of their first meeting. For me, it signaled that my life was out of control. In a very vulnerable way, and without realizing how important it was, I introduced myself as a beginner to this new world of recovery. The beginner mind-set is the only mind-set that is needed for healing to occur. Still, most who attend Twelve Step meetings work hard to get away from the vulnerability of being a beginner. Unless you cultivate a teachable beginner's attitude and maintain it, it is likely that you will relapse or plateau at a place where you feel stymied, or unable to grow in your recovery.

I will never forget my early days of recovery. At the time, I was a practicing minister. I had a lot of theological questions about the Twelve Steps. My sponsor was a kind and gentle man who was not the type to get in your face about dishonesty and denial. Yet, at one point, I shall not forget, he cleared his throat and said, "Ken, I think it would be helpful if you were to be quiet and simply did what you were told." At the time, it hurt my feelings. However, I took his advice, and it saved my life. Because I had determined that I would hock my socks (a phrase that my wife and I created)—which means I will always show up a beginner and go to any lengths necessary to achieve and maintain sobriety and to continue growing—I was able to take his advice and run with it.

For the beginner, in recovery and in life there are many possibilities; for an expert, there are few. I will not leave a Twelve Step meeting until I have received at least one insight that will help me maintain my sobriety and help me to continue to grow. This approach has worked well for me. Yet, it is one of the most difficult mind-sets to maintain. I get tired of searching for tools to help me grow. I also want to see myself as an expert and wise veteran to the ways of recovery. This gets in the way because I tend to get stuck in a sense of pride that complains *I should not have to do now what was at one time required.* For me, adopting a "blue collar" approach to recovery with an emphasis on being hungry for spiritual and recovery growth has helped me to establish long-term relapse maintenance in my recovery from addiction.

Cultivating and maintaining a beginner's mind-set can transform commonplace experience into inner brilliance. But we must be diligent. Do you recall the first day you tried something new? Maybe it was a sport, playing an instrument, or your first day at work at a new job. Can you recall your enthusiasm and willingness to jump in and do whatever was required? You were motivated to do whatever it took to experience the excitement and reward of your new endeavor. The initial excitement often wears thin and soon disappears.

The difficulty about life is that it is daily. It keeps coming at you as long as you are breathing. It is not hard to show up as a beginner when that is what you are. Yet, as time goes by, it is challenging to maintain the intensity and the necessity of a beginner's mind-set. When working a recovery program, maintaining the enthusiasm and hunger for growth is very difficult. Cultivating a beginner's mind-set in ordinary commonplace living is difficult when seeking inner personal brilliance. Community is the container that provides the necessary accountability for doing the work of carving consistency.

Most addicts who suffer chronic relapse do not have a beginner's mind-set. They are unwilling to go to any lengths to end their addictive behavior. I encourage addicts to show up at a

Twelve Step meeting or a sit-down meeting with a sponsor with a beginner's mind-set. And then to do the same in everyday life.

I once worked with a couple of guys who were sex offenders. One, who was a rapist, told me that he was in a situation on a lonely street where there was a single woman who was walking alone. This was an ideal scenario for him to victimize her. He had a strong urge to act out. Yet, to foil his fantasy and plan, he threw his only set of car keys down a storm sewer, eliminating any possibility of escape, and he avoided a relapse and victimizing the woman.

Another guy, a child molester, was sitting in a room with family members who had preschool-age children present. One of the children spontaneously tried to jump onto his lap. This was a very high-risk situation for him. To avoid any possibility of victimizing, he "accidentally" spilled his piping hot coffee into his lap, forcing him to stand up and leave the room.

These two people took relapse prevention seriously and are examples of those who hunger for sobriety and health. It takes this kind of attitude for all of us to grow and establish the kind of mind-set and attitude needed for personal growth in community. The first key to cultivating a dynamic community in everyday living is to establish a beginner's mind-set.

Key #2—Embrace Humility
before You Arrive at the Meeting

Many who first attend Twelve Step meetings show up with an attitude of resistance. They approach the meeting with a "one-down" mentality and an attitude of "coming here to this meeting only confirms that I am a true loser or worse." They miss out on the insights and pearls of wisdom shared by those who are talking about average everyday trials and struggles because they are lost in a false sense of humility that renders them stuck and feeling overwhelmed.

In humility, someone can attend a meeting searching for one insight that can help them remain sober and not leave until they consciously recognize that insight. Further, I can attend the meeting knowing that when I share my own brokenness it will be the very thing that another needs to hear. Just as Bill W. acknowledged "that once when I felt an urge to drink I determined that what I needed was another alcoholic to tell my story."[19] It was in the humble telling that the spark of hunger to remain sober superseded the desire to drink. In this context, the beginner and the veteran can show up as gurus to each other.

I often hear guys say they need a "kickass" therapist or sponsor. I have learned that what is really important is that I become my own "kickass" when needed. This is the same attitude that is necessary in order for anyone to transform commonplace experience into meaningfulness with the help and accountability of community.

Key #3—Cultivate a Listening Spirit

Put yourself in the shoes of the one who is sharing. Listening to what someone else is saying means you must discipline yourself to slow down your expression and tune into the heart of someone else. For so many, this happens so seldom that it seems beyond most of our powers. It means you must make a vigorous effort to

---

19. Bill W., *Alcoholics Anonymous*, 58–71.

zero in to what is being told to you. Being able to connect with community requires listening to what is shared and seeing how it applies to you as opposed to focusing on what does not fit. It is all about attitude.

If you focus on what isn't helpful or necessary, you fuel self-sabotage. Trying to figure out how you do not belong undermines connection. People who do this push away the very source of support they need to save themselves from the throes of addiction. True listening is about connecting with the spirit of the one who is sharing. By doing so, you receive the nugget of wisdom that is there for you.

In order to listen deeply, I must identify with the story being told. The deepest understanding is generated from the position of being equal to the one sharing. We do that through common shared "darkness." It requires that I go deep within my own darkness and embrace painful memories that have been repressed. I need to do this to truly hear the broken voice that is sharing the truth that I need to hear for my healing.

I have attempted to practice this throughout my life when attending Twelve Step meetings and have uncovered a wealth of wisdom that has helped to further my healing. When Michael Brown was killed, I engaged the same principle.

Michael Brown was the eighteen-year-old teenager who was shot and killed by a police officer and left for dead for several hours on a street in Ferguson, Missouri. This event triggered protests and rioting behavior throughout the city that captured the attention of our nation.

Several weeks after the shooting, I traveled to Ferguson in an attempt to connect with the tragic experience so that I might deepen compassion toward those who suffered in this disastrous event. I went to the convenience store where apparently Michael Brown had purchased a Tiparillo cigar. I attempted to reconstruct his walking path down West Florissant Avenue to Canfield Drive. I went to the spot where the memorial was constructed and attempted to visualize what it must have been like for Michael Brown to be hit with the first bullet fired by the officer.

I tried to put myself in the place of Darren Wilson, the officer who shot Brown. I tried to experience what it must have been like for him to have taken another's life. I imagined the fear and the rationale all encompassed in his response.

Then I focused on what the family and folks in the neighborhood must have thought and felt when they realized how long the body had lain in the street before being removed. So much feeling—grief, shock, and deep hurt. As a result of my visit, I believe I was able to connect at a much deeper level of compassion and listen to the much-needed, healing inner wisdom from that experience. Compassion deepens this way.

Key #4—Overcome Fixed Mindedness with an Open Heart

All Indians walk in a single file. At least,
the one I saw was.

—UNKNOWN

Prejudiced thought is often rooted in rigid black-and-white thinking. Broad-brushed conclusions about others happen when we dichotomize the world with a preconceived fixed mind-set. This kind of fixed mindedness diminishes the possibility of getting the most from the group. Buddhist teaching explains that fixed mindedness is a stuck and inflexible thought. It's like living with blinders on.

I have observed members in a Twelve Step community act in ways that suggest the Twelve Step approach is the last word about recovery. Some insist that all you need to do to take care of addiction is read the Big Book and do the Twelve Steps, as if Twelve Step recovery were the final word. Yet even Bill W., cofounder of AA, described an open-ended emphasis on spirituality. He said, "We took the position that AA was not the final word on treatment; that it might be only the first word."

Fear can motivate people to close their heart to other possibilities and approaches to recovery. People sometimes rigidly grasp to what they have out of a fear of letting go. This kind of fixed mindedness undermines their ability to approach a group with an open heart. They tend to be judgmental and maintain rigid conclusions about what should be said and done within the group meeting. Alternate ideas and possibilities are often shut down because of a fixed mind-set.

A fixed mind can stifle and stymy you from exploring the depth of your inner brilliance. Fixed mindedness demands you eliminate the possibility of alternative thinking, which shuts down the brilliance of creative thought and application. Those who embrace a fixed-minded approach to recovery have helped many put a cork in the bottle, stop acting out their addiction, and have saved lives. Yet, with this type of thinking we can miss the brilliance that is present in group recovery that calls us to be authentic and true to our heart. Fixed mindedness narrows our perspective about healing and recovery. An open heart expands our awareness, which is ultimately what helps us deepen our understanding of the healing process.

Healing truth is paradoxical and can be like nailing jelly to a tree. After all is said and done, what is my truth? It can only be known and experienced through an open heart to inner brilliance. With an open-hearted approach toward group meetings, we learn to trust our inner brilliance to figure life out. It requires that we sit with the discomfort of anxiety and uncertainty. As we embrace these unwanted feelings, the brilliance of insightful wisdom will become like the sky. The fettered feelings that distract us will be like clouds that can be cleared to an awakened inner brilliance and wisdom. Living with an open heart is the way to overcome fixed mindedness and helps us gain the most from any support group meeting.

Key #5—Practice the Art of Telling on Yourself

Honesty and transparency make you vulnerable.
Be honest and transparent anyway.
—MOTHER TERESA, The Anyway Poem

Telling on ourselves is a lost art form. Most of us have learned to compensate by living behind a mask that hides authenticity. It has been my experience with church and other religious organizations that authentic truth telling about ourselves is hobbled by beliefs about social expectations. Being open and truthful about destructive behaviors can be unsafe and very costly in these places. I have also found it to be true at times in a Twelve Step community.

For example, if I am an alcoholic and drug addict and I mention a particular stress that triggers the use of both drugs, in some groups I will be reminded that it is okay to talk about the alcohol but not the other drug, because we're in an AA meeting. Or, if I am attending a Sex Addicts Anonymous meeting and I am triggered with arousal to someone in the group, oftentimes it is not okay to talk about the temptation in the group. First, there is a fear for the one who unknowingly is triggering; second, others in the group might be triggered as well. Consequently, being totally honest and transparent is lost in the moment. If it is not safe to talk about a trigger in a Twelve Step group, then where the hell is it safe to talk about the trigger? Alone, so I can fantasize even more?

For me, talking about what triggers destructive behavior with supportive recovering people lowers the intensity of the trigger and helps me manage the intrusive thought. As an addict, I have never needed someone else's creative imagination to devise a way to act out. But I have needed another addict's perspective to intervene on an irrational addictive thought. The triggers have never been about the other person. When I talk about my trigger, I am better able to not objectify an individual or an addictive substance.

When attending a Twelve Step group, I share something about myself I don't want anyone to know. For example, maybe I just acted out and have been lying about my recovery, saying I was sober when I was not. Maybe I just had a huge fight with my wife, or I am jealous or pissed off by someone in the group who did something I did not like. I tell on myself by sharing the last thing I want people to know about me. It is a good warmup toward utilizing the group for what it is designed for—rigorous honesty and vulnerability. It helps me to dispel the ways I try to control what others think of me, and it eases my fear of being real and authentic. -

It is possible to show up at a Twelve Step meeting and hide in the background, particularly when the group is large, and live phony in that community and not be real. But I know how important it is to dispel the bullshit. Only then do I heal through community. Only then can I access my brilliance.

Telling on yourself is the most direct way to cultivate intimacy with self and another, regardless of the relationship. Many community members balk at the idea of telling on themselves. They fear rejection and abandonment if they live and share their truth. The design of a Twelve Step group is to discuss challenges and talk with others who struggle with the same issues to find strength and hope in recovery. When I focus the issue on myself and not another person, the focus becomes me and my share. Being able to share a buildup behavior or a trigger in a safe group is a surefire way of lowering the intensity of craving.

Author David Augsburger developed the term "carefrontation."[20] The idea of carefrontation is to share feedback from a space inside your heart. I care-front others by sharing what I have witnessed or experienced within my own awareness. In this way, I can identify with another person's struggle, and I focus on another person's behavior with sensitivity.

Telling on yourself is a courageous and genuine way to demonstrate self-love, vulnerability, and love toward others. For me, telling on myself has been the best way to avoid isolation and the most direct route toward developing insulation and support from that caring community.

Hillary Clinton was right in her book, *It Takes a Village: And Other Lessons Children Teach Us*. Children do teach us the value of village and community in our effort to heal ourselves. There

---

20. David Augsburger. *Caring Enough to Confront* (Regal Books, 1981), 9.

is brilliance that comes from the dynamic of village. For it truly takes a village to cope with brokenness. When there is a village present, resilience transforms brokenness into healing connection. Twelve step groups are helpful in that they rely on the power of mutual community. When people embrace hunger and humility, listen openly and become transparent with each other, community becomes a powerful healing village.

Questions

1. Can you identify a community you feel connected with through common shared brokenness?

2. What would you need to change within yourself to create a beginner's mind-set within the community that you feel accountable to?

3. There's an old saying: "If eight people tell you that you have a tail, the least you would do is look at your ass in the mirror." What issues are you defensive about when confronted by your support community?

4. What issue in your life are you fix-minded about, and who would you be willing to tell on yourself about this issue?

Chapter 6

Living with Loneliness and Making It Meaningful

*Loneliness is and always has been the central
and inevitable experience of every man.*
—Thomas Wolfe

I t's true. Loneliness touches the lives of everybody. Whether we are rich and famous or lost and forgotten, the experience of loneliness invades us all. Mother Teresa said, "One of the greatest diseases is to be nobody to anybody."

Intense loneliness hurts in every part of your body. It can cause panic and the deepest heartache you will ever know. Yet, none of us, addicts or otherwise, will get through life without experiencing its impact. Loneliness is universal. Even my dog knows the feeling of being lonely.

Loneliness and depression go together. The pervasive experience of loneliness in our society correlates with increased rates of depression. Studies show a decrease in close friends, the kind of confidante with whom we can freely discuss personal matters. According to *Live Science* reporter Robert Roy Britt, from 1985 to 2004, the number of close friends a typical person has dropped from three to two. We have never been so socially connected yet so isolated and lonely in our culture. We have Facebook, LinkedIn, Twitter, Instagram, Snapchat, and other social media options to connect our lives in a myriad of ways. Yet, I have a hunch that each of these has its own way of isolating and fueling loneliness and depression.

Actor and comedian Brett Gelman said, "I've definitely had long stretches of time in my personal life where I've felt an intense loneliness and a desperation to feel something real and to have something that truly meant something in my life." According to Sara Knapton, science editor of the *Telegraph*, this desperation and intense loneliness can kill. Some experts claim that loneliness attributes to a 14 percent increase in earlier deaths. Loneliness makes cancer deadlier and causes Alzheimer's to advance faster. A 2010 AARP study reported that loneliness is twice as deadly as obesity and as deadly as smoking a pack of cigarettes a day.[21] Once loneliness becomes chronic, it can become self-sustaining.

Kids can be lonely too. Civil rights activist Ruby Bridges was the first African American to desegregate an all-white elementary

---

21. AARP Loneliness Study. *"Loneliness Rivals Obesity, Smoking as Health Risk."* May 4, 2018. https://www.webmd.com/balance/news/20180504/loneliness-rivals-obesity-smoking-as-health-risk

school in New Orleans. She said, "What I remember about first grade was that it was very lonely. I didn't have any friends, and I wasn't allowed to go to the cafeteria or play on the playground. What bothered me most was the loneliness in school every day."[22]

I also grew up a lonely kid. Even though I grew up in a family of nine kids and my parents raised my oldest sister's three children, loneliness persisted.

There was a lot of physical, emotional, sexual, and religious abuse in my family. To cope and survive, I learned to create solitary games to escape the pain and isolation from the abuse. No one ever crawled inside my head to figure out what made me tick. If someone had, they would have found a very lonely and bored kid who carried the weight of the world on his shoulders while being riddled with anxiety. As a young boy, I developed an imaginary friend. I used to go on long walks and talk with my imaginary friend who I thought understood me and would comfort me. By doing this, I got through the elementary school years.

Loneliness is pervasive. It is a common experience that all of humanity can identify with. Those who dare to explore average must dare to recognize and embrace loneliness. Rich and famous people can't escape loneliness either. Many celebrities have shared a tragic story of depression and loneliness. Even when you are world renowned, the world you live in is limited.

You may think everyone knows about your fear of being lonely. Yet, when Tiger Woods was going through his infamous, excruciatingly painful public experience of marital infidelity that involved his own struggle with loneliness, the Dalai Lama was asked to comment about Tiger's dilemma. Awkwardly, he remarked, "Who is Tiger Woods?"

---

22. Ruby Bridges. *Through My Eyes*, (New York: Scholastic Press, 1999).

Actor Tom Hanks commented, "Everybody has something that chews them up and, for me, that thing was always loneliness." He later added, "The cinema has the power to make you not feel lonely, even when you are." Actress Liv Ullmann said, "Hollywood is loneliness beside the swimming pool." Author Johann Hari reported that 50 percent of people who were asked who they would reach out to if they were facing a crisis responded, "Nobody."

Without question, loneliness is a common component of addiction. Through all the years of working with addicts, I have yet to encounter one who was not dominated by loneliness when acting out. My mentor and colleague, Dr. Ralph Earle, wrote a book about sex addiction called *Lonely All the Time*. It underscores the basic fuel of every addict I have ever treated.

Causation

I wake up with my stomach churning and a lump in my throat. I put my jeans on and find my shoes. I shake my head because I feel the brain fog messing with my perspective and permeating my Monday morning with gloom. It is also draining my energy for my regular morning workout. After making some coffee, I sit in the quietness of the morning. I listen to the birds singing their usual song and the normal morning sounds that occur in and around my house.

When I stand up to get a cup of coffee, the blood rushes out of my head—I feel faint. My knees are stiff and sore and I tell myself it's a bummer getting old. After pouring a cup, I sit back down in my chair and take inventory from the inside of my guts. I recognize I feel somewhat weary; emotionally empty; physically fatigued; a tinge of anxiety, despair, depression; and a lot of loneliness.

My hunch is that this description is true of a lot of folks not only on Monday mornings but every workday morning. There is a powerful combination of difficult feelings that hit a lot of people with sadness and loneliness every morning. For me, I ask the question, "Why?" After all, I have a good job, enough money to retire, a wife who loves me and who I love, adult children who are working to fulfill their dreams, and at the age of sixty-eight, I feel pretty healthy. Why would I feel down with loneliness with this kind of life description? Isn't this sort of what we mapped out thirty years ago when we thought of what sixty-eight would look like with our families?

I am lucky to be so emotionally rich, healthy, and well off. Many people are not healthy, they don't have enough money to retire, their adult children are not doing all that well, and most of the dreams they wanted to pursue have long since evaporated like clouds in their coffee. When these are the realities, optimism and enthusiasm for life fade and the shadow of loneliness creeps in. Woody Allen reflected the perspective of so many when he said, "Life is full of misery, loneliness, and suffering—and it's all over much too soon."

There are many reasons why loneliness is so prevalent. Human experience entails disappointment, heartache, failure, and loss. Losing a relationship is always difficult and sometimes devastating. Most of us have had the experience of being really close to someone and then having that person become distant. It can be very painful. There are times when people seem to walk alongside and commune with us and we grow fond of their friendship—even learn to love them. Then, as life unfolds, they go away and walk another path. Letting go of those precious relationships can be very difficult and trigger painful feelings of desertion.

We tend to want to pull back and avoid the fear of abandonment, even when it is a common relational dynamic of living in community. We do what we can to avoid feeling lonely and rejected. The more we grasp and try to hold on, the more likely we sink into the throes of debilitating loneliness and isolation.

Struggle and failure accelerate separation from community. Whenever I failed to fulfill an expectation, it was such an empty feeling. I felt the intense loneliness deep within. Sometimes it was so deep that I didn't want anyone else to know it or touch it. It can make me a stranger in my own house because I don't want anyone to know just how bad it hurts.

The disappointment that comes from poor results can trigger isolation and intense loneliness. Yet we all fail. Consequently, we must learn to navigate loneliness. Failure sparks shame and withdrawal from support and community. I want to tell myself that there is something wrong with me and the poor result is proof. I conclude that I am flawed more than others, and I don't belong or deserve to connect with those who are perceived as successful people. As a result, I isolate and increase my experience of loneliness.

Betrayal

Is there anything lonelier than betrayal? If we live long enough, we will experience the paralyzing impact of relational betrayal, one way or another. It may be promises broken by a friend or a breach of contract in a business relationship. Perhaps the most harrowing and horrible betrayal is when a partner in a personal relationship lies, cheats, and is unfaithful. It may feel like a living death. Life becomes surreal.

Heartache invades whenever those we love and care for are touched with human tragedy. And a broken heart can be more serious than you might think. Over the course of five years, researchers from Harvard interviewed 2,000 patients who suffered from heart attacks. Some of the questions involved triggering events. The results showed the risk of heart attack is eight times higher than normal during the week after the death of a loved one. Heart attacks from heartbreak are among the many common life experiences that we all must learn to manage.[23]

Disappointment

Disappointment is an everyday reality. Disappointment stimulates the parasympathetic nervous system. There is a chemical response that results in melancholy, inertia, and a feeling of hopelessness. Unresolved disappointment can cause tiredness, numbing sensations, sweating, diarrhea, and even an increased heart rate. Diseases can show up when life gets hectic and you are stressed for a pronounced period of time. Heart disease, digestive disorders, and a depressed immune system are all possible. Disappointment triggers despondency and activates intense loneliness, particularly when it goes unchecked.

Ambiguous Loss

Pauline Boss is credited with identifying and raising the consciousness level around the need to grieve ambiguous loss, sometimes referred to as disenfranchised grief. Her book *Ambiguous Loss: Learning to Live with Unresolved Grief* explains the isolation

---

23. Murray A. Mittleman and Elizabeth Mostofsky. "Physical, Psychological and Chemical Triggers of Acute Cardiovascular Events." *Circulation: Journal of the American Heart Association* (July 2011):346-354. https://ahajournals.org/doi/full/10.1161/circulationaha.110.968776?sid=6185a6c6-e9a2-4ab3-9b14-ac7c94decfbd

and loneliness that exists when grief never ends. Perhaps the most stressful and lonely loss of all is when there is no real possibility of a sense of physical closure. This happens when you cannot be sure whether your loved one is still alive.

Experts in healing grief suggest there is never any real final closure with death and other excruciating losses. When there is an unclear loss, the physicality of loss is always pending. It becomes very difficult to move forward. People who suffer sexual abuse and families whose loved ones succumb to Alzheimer's, addiction, and other serious mental illnesses all experience ambiguous loss. While the world goes on, it is easy to fall into isolation and loneliness fueled by the reality of ambiguous loss.

Materialism

A sex addict whose longest binge with pornography was sixty hours told me, "I can't get enough of what I really don't want." Sixty hours is about 2.5 days of porn nonstop! I have heard many other bizarre and extended sexual pursuits and other out-of-control, insatiable conquests coming from addictive urges. The greatest of these is the lust for power, possession, and position. The disease of "more" has not only wrecked people's lives but has left addicts and untold millions of others paralyzed with loneliness.

In Johann Hari's book about depression, *Lost Connections*, he recognizes junk values as products or services that are being marketed to you that boast of solutions for happiness. He claims that just as junk food can take over your diet, junk values can take over your mind. It's as if you cannot be satisfied until you possess the latest electronics or fastest cars. Yet the more you are driven for material success, the shallower your life becomes and the more loneliness persists.

Childhood Trauma

The worst loneliness is not to be comfortable with yourself.

—Mark Twain

When you experience childhood trauma, you need to heal from it. Childhood trauma has a way of contaminating the essence of who you are. You just feel dirty, used, and forever flawed. According to Dr. Vincent Felitti, who coordinated a study that measured the impact of childhood trauma in more than 17,000 participants, the greater and more complicated the Adverse Childhood Experience (ACE), the more likelihood of suffering from a myriad of mental illnesses, maladaptive response behaviors, and long-term chronic loneliness.[24]

Many people who have suffered major childhood traumas miss out on getting key childhood developmental needs met. Children have many emotional needs that must be met by their parents. Caregivers are responsible for the guidance and cultivation of the physical, intellectual, emotional, and moral development of their child. When this doesn't happen, childhood development becomes like a chunk of Swiss cheese with the holes in it. The holes represent the unmet needs. To fill the hole, the child often reaches outside to another person or experience.

For example, children can know their mother and father love them because the parents provide shelter, food, clothing, and education. However, as noted earlier, they only learn they matter when parents spend sufficient amounts of time with them on their terms. When this does not happen, children subconsciously

---

24. Jill Levenson. "Adverse Childhood Experiences and Subsequent Substance Abuse in a Sample of Sexual Offenders: Implications for Treatment and Prevention," Victims & Offenders, no. 11(2):1-26.

learn that their sense of being is not as important. To know they matter, children look to see what matters to their parents and concentrate their focus there. A child may excel in academics, sports, band, church, a scout program, or working hard. Subconsciously, they do whatever it takes to get the caregiver's attention to know that they matter. At this stage in life, loneliness and abandonment is far too painful and risky.

In *The Drama of the Gifted Child*, author Alice Miller speaks to the impact of loneliness for children who do not get their significant developmental needs met. She writes, "Quite often I have been faced with people who were praised and admired for their talents and their achievements, who were toilet trained in the first year of their lives, and who may even, at the age of one and a half to five, have capably helped to take care of their younger siblings. According to prevailing attitudes, these people—the pride of their parents—should have had a strong and stable sense of self-assurance. But the case is exactly the opposite.

"They do well, even excellently, in everything they undertake; they are admired and envied; they are successful whenever they care to be—but behind all this lurks depression and chronic loneliness leading to a sense that life has no meaning. These dark feelings will come to the fore as soon as the drug of grandiosity fails, as soon as they are not "on top," not definitely the "superstar," or whenever they suddenly get the feeling they have failed to live up to some ideal image or have not measured up to some standard. Then they are plagued by anxiety or deep feelings of guilt, shame and loneliness."[25]

Loneliness can be caused by a myriad of contributing factors. Once you identify the causes of your loneliness, you are positioned

---

25. Alice Miller. Drama of the Gifted Child (New York: Basic Books, 2008), 5.

to replace loneliness with solitude—and to transform it into your personal brilliance.

How to Manage Loneliness and Make it Meaningful

If you go deeper and deeper into your own heart, you'll be living in a world with less fear, isolation and loneliness.

—Sharon Salzberg

Pray that your loneliness may spur you into finding something to live for, great enough to die for.

—Dag Hammarskjold

In my nearly thirty years of treating addiction, I have yet to hear a story of acting out or a relapse behavior that did not include extreme loneliness. It's a common experience among recovering addicts. Those who establish sobriety and have serenity have learned to manage their loneliness and find meaning in it.

Does it make sense to embrace the experience of loneliness? Some believe that it would be better to eliminate loneliness whenever it appears. Paradoxically, those who have been willing to embrace loneliness and sit with it can deepen the meaning of life. The following five steps will help you make meaningfulness from loneliness.

#1 Dare to Be Vulnerable

Lean into the pain that you most want to avoid. We are creatures designed for connection, and we find this connection in community. Yet, we all have attended and belonged to organizations, church or otherwise, where we have felt profound loneliness even though we are conversing, smiling, and engaging with others. In these types of settings, we often attempt to connect through common shared strengths. We look for the sports enthusiast, the automobile buff, common shared business practices, or anything else so we can feel that connection.

For most people, social settings that tend to remain stuck in small talk have a short shelf life. We are designed to meet our need for belonging by going deeper in our conversations. Human beings connect with each other in healthy ways by sharing the reality of shared weaknesses. When we are connected to each other through common shared weakness, we are not threatened by each other's strength. Rather, we rejoice with them as they rejoice with us in our strengths. These are the average experiences of life that cultivate the brilliance of connection.

Take the risk of becoming emotionally naked by sharing raw emotions. Acknowledge what others may view as a weakness. Intimacy is about taking this risk. It means I am willing to show my vulnerable insides, knowing full well that you may say "thanks, but no thanks." The challenge is to lean into this opportunity of deepening heart-to-heart connection in the presence of possible rejection.

In case you were wondering, the idea isn't to break the ice at a social party by suddenly announcing that you wet the bed until you were in fifth grade or you learned about masturbation with your Dad's porn stash and your parents' dildo! Likely, we have all had conversations with people who seem to spill their guts all too soon. There is a difference from this kind of exhibitionistic share and being real and authentic. Authentic sharing with an open heart is medicine to the soul of those who suffer from loneliness.

The idea of men being vulnerable by crying is commonly spurned in our culture, where emphasis is placed on men protecting their "man card" with machismo by denying vulnerable emotions such as fear and sadness. Most men don't feel safe or even know how to express authentic feelings. This is where image control comes up. Often, men are encouraged to "man up" which usually means to be stoic and pretend to be tough. Of course, men are encouraged to embrace one feeling—anger. That is okay to express. In our culture, anger promotes power and manhood. It is common for people to believe that a man is weak if he chooses to be vulnerable with his tears. Tears are something to be shared in isolation.

Some women would agree that men being vulnerable with their emotions is unattractive; it makes them look weak. However, throughout the years of my relational work with men and women, regardless of sexual orientation, this doesn't hold true. The vast majority seek enriched intimacy with their partner and long for them to courageously open their heart and express genuine feelings—other than just anger—whatever they are.

I have conducted about 200 weekend retreats with men who are addicts. The magic occurs when men put aside the bullshit and the image management and share deep from within their heart their fears, sadness, and loneliness. By daring to be vulnerable, they discover a caring bond, otherwise unknown. The intensity of pervading chronic loneliness lifts, and the result is an understanding of how to find a meaningful replacement. During these retreats, men cry uncontrollably, shake with fear, and express their deepest genuine anger about childhood abandonment and receive unconditional acceptance from their peers.

These men walk away knowing the value of expressing vulnerability. They see the courage it takes to confront their loneliness. Leaning into the pain of lonely living creates resolution. It makes the average day meaningful. Loneliness, then, is a conduit for healing. Admitting to being lonely adds brilliance to an average experience. Dare to be vulnerable!

#2 Sit with Silent Places in Your Life and Let Them Speak to You

When things get quiet and we can almost hear our heart thumping in our chest, we tend to create some kind of noise to take us away from these silent places. Yet, silence is necessary to transforming loneliness into meaningfulness.

The silence of loneliness can be a way to best see things for what they are. It can tell you so much about yourself and the world around you. Catholic theologian, Henri Nouwen, emphasized that sitting with the lonely quiet places in life creates a movement from a restless sense to a restful spirit, or into a garden of solitude.

#3 Learn to Grieve Deeply and Do It Well

Life is a tapestry of highs and lows, successes and failures, and hellos and good-byes. Loneliness is a message about grief and loss. It comes with the loss of friends and family through death or destruction in relationship. Grieving is a common experience to everyone. Yet, few of us are taught to grieve deeply. Most of us don't have a good role model for what effective grieving and mourning looks like.

Consequently, most people withdraw from grieving through avoidance strategies and try to present a positive front. Many are taught to maintain a "stiff upper lip" and remain on task with life through busyness. Others fall through the cracks of society trying to numb out depressing sadness with alcohol, drugs, or other addictions. Our society allows for a certain season of time for grieving death and loss but then impatiently insists that those who grieve must move on. Yet, truth and reality attest that grieving never ends as long as we are in this world. When there is significant loss, closure never occurs.

To grieve deeply is to shift from a focus of closure around loss to actively grieving. It is a characteristic of emotional growth and maturity. Healing involves validating our hurtful sad memories without trying to fix or take ourselves away from sadness. In time, the intensity of the sadness lifts, and we move on, allowing the sadness to be in our hearts.

With significant loss, the mourning will surface from time to time. Rather than allow the mourning to dominate our life, we can allow the grief to flow freely and feel the deep sense of richness and healing that comes from embracing grief. We are designed to embrace the depth of anguish and anxiety that grief brings and then release this deep pain, letting it flow out of our bodies and lives. The amount of time this takes depends upon the complexity of loss experienced. When there is a community that patiently supports and validates the mourner, those who grieve are able to move forward with a deeper perspective on life.

#4 Commit to Making Everyday Adjustments

Loneliness can be a transmitter signaling a need that must be met in a healthy way. Sitting with loneliness and listening to its message can help you make adjustments necessary to achieve life balance. For addicts, unstructured and unaccounted for time can prove to be high risk. When alone, emptiness and loneliness often creep in. Stress and pressure spark cravings for escape during alone moments.

Triggered by painful past times of abandonment, addicts often seek avoidance by numbing out with their drug of choice. However, addicts who learn to bend with flexibility and go with the flow of whatever life brings, can find meaningfulness in loneliness. They don't break from its heaviness. They learn to sit with the discomfort and learn how to be all alone with their feelings. By writing about their feelings, they can become relieved. They can learn to reach out to someone and discover how soothing it is to have an uneventful conversation with another human being who also understands what it means to feel lonely. In this way, rather than running in fear from loneliness, it becomes a signal that can direct self-care. It's all part of the process of growing ourselves up emotionally.

#5 Give Up the Story Line—You Are Not Your Past

Activist and educator Angela Davis took the Serenity Prayer and announced, "I am no longer accepting the things I cannot change. I am changing the things I cannot accept." Loneliness does not have to be permanent. The cycle of loneliness can self-sabotage us.

When loneliness is chronic, the brain goes into self-defense. It looks for hostility everywhere, assumes the worst about the intentions of others, and triggers a cold response to the world. Once you embrace the grief, do not to wallow in the dregs of mistaken belief about yourself. Once you have looked backward and gained precious understanding, it's important to move forward.

You do not have to remain stuck in yesterday's story line. Yesterday ended last night and you are not who, what, or where you were yesterday. There comes a time to take action. You can choose to insulate with others in the community and not isolate; to not personalize another's behavior toward you or close your heart to them. There is a time to check things out and remain open hearted, even if you are hurting.

When you feel isolated, write a friend you have not spoken to. Reach out to an estranged family member. Share your feelings even when you don't want to. Listen to someone who needs to say some things that may be critical and be big enough to validate their perspective. Refuse to accept critical mistaken beliefs you tell yourself and always practice self-affirmations.

When you change how you see things in a relationship, you begin to move away from a deprived mind-set that suggests you are not worthy of getting your needs met. Giving up the story line requires that each of us recognizes that loneliness is a part of average everyday living, and we have the privilege of making meaningfulness out of our lonely experiences.

Enlightenment from Everyday Living

Average, everyday life experiences are necessary to access inner brilliance. Ignoring those ordinary places or writing them off as unimportant eliminates the potential of going deep within yourself to mature and form brilliance. Focusing on spectacular results from achieving specific goals is superficial in the absence of going deep. It's the undistinguished, unexceptional moment so mainstream to all that ties together the bitter with sweet and the triumph with defeat. Brilliance is formed in the process of sifting and sorting ordinary struggle in typical mundane moments of daily living.

Embracing everyday living leads you to your true self. Tolerance and forgiveness are familiar life experiences with promise to transform and create brilliance from brokenness. To achieve this, you must be willing to lean into the depth and breadth of where forgiveness and tolerance will lead. Sorrow is a prevalent experience throughout all of life that promotes depth and maturity. Obscurity and boredom are prosaic moments for all that must be embraced for life to have matter and meaningfulness.

Questions

1. Reflect on times during your childhood and adult life when you felt your loneliest. During those times, how did you try to cope with your loneliness? Share your experiences with a close friend.

2. Each of the following categories are cause for loneliness. Reflect on how you managed the loneliness in each experience:

    a. Disappointment:
    b. Heartache:
    c. Failure:
    d. Ambiguous loss:

3. Circle the solutions toward managing loneliness you have struggled with the most:

   a. Dare to be vulnerable, or lean into the pain that you would most like to avoid

   b. Sit with the silent places of your life and let them speak to you

   c. Learn to grieve deeply and to do it well

   d. Commit to making everyday adjustments

   e. Give up the story line; you are not your past

Chapter 7

Going Deep—Being Your Authentic, True Self

*Soul is about authenticity. Soul is about finding
the things in your life that are real and pure.*

—JOHN LEGEND

I like to think of myself as a frank, forthright, and honest soul. Yet, the most difficult journey I have ever made was going below the surface of everyday thought into the deep caverns of my heart. To demonstrate transparent honesty in those places, to embrace the intimidating and sometimes ugly truth about reality, has always been a difficult struggle for me. However, without going deep in the pursuit of my personal truth about life and the world around me, it would seem like being an Olympic swimmer confined to an inflatable kiddie pool trying to figure out creative ways to use water wings.

Being able to navigate the surface has always been utilitarian and helpful. Daring to embrace the often-overlooked average, commonplace experiences of life and go deep has added the rich reward of meaningfulness to my life.

Going deep includes embracing paradox. At times it means knowing when to quit, even coming to terms with personal limits, realizing you can't do or have it all. It can feel like bushwhacking in an uncharted thick forest. Going deep always takes you beyond your comfort zone. It can be like going on an outdoor adventure with the most meaningful part being you sitting under a tree watching an ant crawl up your leg while you contemplate the possibility of connecting to your finite obscurity. In the end, going deep is essentially about coming home to yourself and learning to be true to your heart.

Going Deep with Authenticity

Robert Crichton wrote about the all-time great imposter Ferdinand Demara in his book, *The Great Imposter*. Amazingly, Demara was able to impersonate as a civil engineer, a lawyer, a sheriff's deputy, a Benedictine monk, a prison warden, and the dean of psychology at Gannon College, all without ever having achieved a high school diploma. His greatest impersonation was fraudulently posing as his close friend, Dr. Joseph Cyr. He stole his identification and then signed himself on as a doctor for the Royal Canadian Navy. While on a Royal Canadian Navy destroyer, he faced his greatest imposter challenge. Nineteen serious casualties in the

Korean War needed immediate attention and surgery. The following is his March 16, 1951, diary entry:

It was not necessary to make me aware of the mess of bodies. I saw them as soon as we pulled up alongside a boat with casualties. I ran at a moderate pace down to the engine room to collect my thoughts. I was silently hoping that in my absence the men would figure out a solution on their own. But alas, they found me. I had no choice but to rise to the occasion. I quickly instructed my medical assistant, Hotchin, to get all of the wounded men aboard our ship. There were nineteen wounded Korean soldiers in all, and three of them were seriously hurt. Each of them would die within the next 24 hours unless they received surgery. I decided to start with the lightly wounded first, in hopes that the seriously wounded ones would pass away before I would have to figure out how to operate on them. Looking back on yesterday's events, I realize that was a morbid hope, but I had no time to reflect on personal morality with the lives of nineteen men in my untrained hands.

Everyone was looking at me. In all my years of assuming false identities, I had never before felt like such an imposter and a fraud. There was no way to dodge this and no place to run to. What happened next was nothing short of a straight-from-heaven miracle. With my limited knowledge of medicine and generous amounts of penicillin, I was able to clean, clamp, and suture sixteen of the men into healthy and stable conditions. I then ordered the crew to disinfect a cabin to the best of their abilities so that I could use it as an operating room for the three men who needed major surgery. Who knows how long Hotchin, the captain, and I spent in that cabin. It felt like days.

For the first time in my entire life I performed major surgery. I used tools I had never even heard of before, such as a bone saw and a rib spreader. I even witnessed a man's bare beating heart right before my eyes...

Of those nineteen men, miraculously, not a single one died. I stumbled back to my cabin that night and slept for almost a full day. I feel as if I am writing about a dream. Everything happened so fast, and there were so many bodies; any average Joe would deem yesterday more fit for dreamland than the real world.[26]

Feeling Like a Fraud

One of the common disclosures that I hear from addicts is the experience of feeling like a fraud. The Dr. Jekyll and Mr. Hyde experience of addiction leaves an addict painfully lonely and hollow inside and feeling like an imposter. This would be true of anyone, not just addicts. The longing to be authentic and true to oneself is a common thirst and hunger among all. As novelist Richard Rohr put it, "We all would like to find the true shape of our own self."[27]

There is always a struggle to separate what your True Self is from your False Self. True Self is what you really are, that unrepeatable miracle of God. It is that divine DNA about you, your organic wholeness, which is manifested in your destiny. The False Self is the image you put forward in impression management. It can be promoted by way of your vocation, what you wear, where you live, who you know, and how you live. It falls short of being

26. Ferdinand Demara. *The Great Imposter.* New York: Random House, 1959.
27. Richard Rohr. *Immortal Diamond.* San Francisco, CA: Jossey-Bass, 2013.

the real genuine you. Our False Self identifies with imposters such as Ferdinand Demara because when we are not our True Self, we feel just as inadequate and ill-equipped as he did when treating those patients.

It has been my experience that when you are real and genuine, you feel and even fit better in your own skin. Like in *The Velveteen Rabbit*, the Skin Horse told the rabbit —the "real" never rubs off, it lasts forever.[28] A False Self is never truly satisfying. It triggers addiction and the need to keep trying to be more to keep from being less. The False Self makes a person hyper vigilant from a fear of being caught not measuring up. It triggers people to get stuck with image management. When you ground yourself in your genuine, authentic True Self, you let go of these anxiety-producing behaviors. You feel more at peace.

The greatest challenge to the True Self is living an incongruent life. When what I feel is different from what I say and what I do, I can get stuck in incongruent living. Everyone is incongruent sometime. But when it happens over and over again, this spells trouble as you begin living a double life. This is the dilemma that an addict must unravel in order to establish consistent long-term sobriety. When what an addict thinks and values is in tune with what he feels, this begins to harmonize with what he says and does, resulting in sobriety and serenity.

To accomplish this mind-set, you need to manage paradox. While congruent living is the goal, the reality is that everyone is inconsistent, incongruent, and hypocritical in some ways. I have not known an addict in recovery who has always been consistent with every recovery task. For many people, confusion and uncertainty trigger incongruent living and hypocrisy. The footprint of

28. Margery Williams. *The Velveteen Rabbit*, New York: Doubleday, 1991

hypocrisy treads through everyone's life. Sometimes the impact is major or at times less so. It underscores the human condition.

When incongruent, inconsistent, or hypocritical behavior appears, you'll want to have someone or a group hold you accountable. The strength of accountability keeps human weakness in check and can be humbling when the reality of shortcomings sets in. So, rather than impersonate sobriety or serenity, an addict in recovery can humbly confess their shortcomings knowing that the power of accountability will call them back to a centered, congruent life. To preserve your True Self, practice telling on yourself.

At a Twelve Step meeting, once you tell everyone your deepest, darkest, most shameful secret and feel the acceptance of those attending, it is difficult to return and tell the same people that the behavior you committed to not doing—you did again. There is a fear of rejection and embarrassment even though you are in a room full of addicts. If you have had weeks or years of sobriety, have become a sponsor or a trusted servant in the meetings, there is even greater fear of rejection if you need to honestly disclose that you have been acting out against your values.

It is difficult to tell on yourself. Yet it is absolutely necessary in order to establish congruency. Beyond the confession, what is required is a commitment to self and to the group that you will do whatever it takes to recenter and live a sober life. You need to do this to find your True Self.

Although being your True Self takes hard work, it is the only way to establish the confidence needed to build an authentic foundation for long-term recovery. When you are trying to be centered and remain sober and true to your heart, there are many distractions to pull you away from focused living and back to your addiction. I face a number of decisions about groups that I lead, individual clients that I see, and relationships that I encounter that can pull me away from being true to my heart. I fear rejection if I tell others my truth, which may not align with what they want to hear from me. I might make decisions about group processes that could be shortsighted or reactionary. Some of these decisions I may later regret. I might disappoint someone with an action that I choose to do or a boundary that I set.

Ultimately, I fear disapproval of others, which will leave me feeling emotionally abandoned. Like many, I want to avoid the conflict, dread, and anxiety that causes a lot of nervous energy, whether noticed by others or not. As my emotions build up around several issues, I can become vulnerable to a desire to escape. There is no more surefire way to escape than by numbing out with drugs or addictive behavior. When I give in to acting out, that is when I lose my True Self because I am no longer being true to my heart. Instead, I become lost in a sea of growing confusion with more of the feelings I was trying to escape. It can then quickly spiral into a vortex of negative emotions, leaving me feeling empty and hollow inside. Very quickly I feel fraudulent like the imposter Ferdinand Demara.

In the movie *Yesterday*, Jack Malik is a struggling singer-songwriter in an English seaside town. His dreams of fame are rapidly fading. After a freak bus accident during a mysterious global blackout, Jack wakes up to discover that The Beatles have never existed. Performing songs by the greatest band in history to a world that has never heard them, Jack becomes an overnight sensation.

As the story line unfolds, he can't live with himself and the hollow feeling that comes from living the life of an imposter. The anxiety and loneliness build to a crisis until he is able to confess his impersonation to the only couple in all the world who knows the truth. Only when he confesses that he is an imposter to thousands of people at a concert does he find his True Self.

Eventually, he returns to his hometown and plays in front of a local school party. Gone is the fanfare and fame of thousands of admirers. Although the kids attending don't notice, Jack has found himself once again by being true to himself. In the end, he found serenity by choosing to be true to his heart.

For all of us, the challenge to embrace our True Self with a firm grip is never easy. It is a common space that impacts everyone. Those who choose to be true to themselves truly experience the joy of their own brilliance.

Questions

1. Describe a time in your life when you felt like an impersonator.

2. In what ways have you personally experienced being inconsistent, incongruent, and hypocritical?

3. How has being accountable to someone or some group helped you to be true to yourself?

Chapter 8

Going Deep—
Embracing Tolerance
and Forgiveness

Forgiveness is not always easy. At times, it feels
more painful than the wound we suffered,
to forgive the one that inflicted it. And yet,
there is no peace without forgiveness.

—MARIANNE WILLIAMSON

On Wednesdays, I conduct a Spirituality group. A handful of people usually attend. They are patients engaged in an intensive process for one to two weeks. Each Wednesday, there are different folks attending. Inevitably, I begin the group session by asking, "What does spirituality mean to you?" Many respond with passion and conviction about their religious faith. I follow up with the question, "How does your understanding of spirituality help you when you are stuck in your destructive behavior?" The responses vary but often include what spirituality should do rather than what it actually does. By asking this question it allows them to examine their beliefs.

Spirituality is not necessary to love those who love me. If I cannot love those who love me, then my problem is more psychological than spiritual. Most organized religions promote that you are to love those who hate or those who might be considered an enemy. The Dalai Lama remarked, "We have the most to learn from our enemies. In a way they are our best teachers."

This is where it becomes conditional, complicated, and difficult. Marianne Williamson is correct to declare that forgiveness is not always easy. When hatred, division, and strife exist, forgiveness can seem impossible. Families who experience genocide, generations of racial prejudice, and many other forms of gnarly tragic circumstances perpetrated by those with greed and hate face impossible conditions in which to consider forgiveness.

Our country is fraught with division and intolerance. Mass shootings, racial intolerance, social injustice, pro life versus pro choice, and immigration issues fuel attitudes of intolerance. Healing requires tolerance and maturity. Tolerance is not just putting up with another person's differences or idiosyncrasies. It means to care and identify with someone who is different and disagreeable. Tolerance multiplies appreciation for the rich diversity that exists on the earth and promotes the deep understanding that all our struggles are the same. It is possible to connect to the same fears, the same sorrows.

Most folks are doing the best they can to make life work out. In his book *His Holiness*, the Dalai Lama made this appeal to the world: "On some days I think it would be better if there were no religions. All religions and all scriptures harbor potential for violence. This is why we need secular ethics beyond all religions. It is more important for schools to have classes on ethics other than religion. Why? Because it's more important to be aware of our commonalities than to constantly emphasize what divides us."[29] This spirit points to the common threads of everyday living that connects humanity.

I have always thought of forgiveness as a litmus test for religious people. Tolerance moves beyond connection with others whom we share commonality. Connecting through weakness brings people together and is often where we find our bond and common beginnings. In their book, *Spirituality of Imperfection*, authors Kurtz and Ketcham wrote, "There is no community without that which is flawed and imperfect. When weakness is not shared, then strength becomes a threat."[30]

Over the years, the men who have committed to the Twelve Step–group weekends that I have led quickly learn the value of a common shared story of brokenness. It is not the acting out behavior that is common to another but the story line of shared vulnerability. Around kitchen tables, campfires, fireplaces, and living rooms, men have shared with tears the agony, loneliness, and emptiness resulting from out-of-control behavior. Somehow the courage to share from the depth of heart creates a healing

---

29. Dalai Lama. *An Appeal to the World: The Way to Peace in a Time of Division.* (New York: William Morrow, 2017).

30. Earnest Kurtz and Katherine Ketchum. *The Spirituality of Imperfection: Storytelling and the Search for Meaning* (New York: Bantam, 1993).

salve of tolerance, not for the behavior but for the person in the brokenness.

Everyone who sits in the circle of vulnerability knows the intensity of shared emotional pain. This dynamic has drawn men to come back again and again—to gather around in a circle to listen to the fascinating story of common shared brokenness. Countless times I have heard "to listen to this person's powerful story in overcoming brokenness inspires me and fuels hope that I, too, can find my way. I can respect where we are different because I can connect with where we are alike!" Humanity fosters bonding among people who have gone through the same ordeal, struggle, and crisis.

How to Cultivate Tolerance

Tolerance is the first principle of community; it is the spirit which conserves the best that all men think.

—HELEN KELLER

The ingredients for tolerance can be summed up in the acronym VOCAL. To create tolerance, you need a sense of Vision (V); a willingness to be Open (O) to differences; Cooperation (C), not competition; Acceptance (A) of other people's power; and the capacity to Listen (L) to the heart of self and others.

Tolerance begins with a Vision. John Lennon imagined a world with no countries, nothing to kill or die for, no religion, no heaven, no hell, a world that lives as one. He was well aware that he was often labeled a dreamer. He was confident that he was not the only one to embrace this vision of tolerance. For sure he was not.

Vision Is Inspired Thought

What we think about expands our reality. If you envision tolerance, cooperation, and acceptance toward all, that is what will expand. We're all capable of having this capacity. Consider the following:

- What would the world be like if countries reached out to one another and made sure that those who were hungry were fed and those who were devastated by natural disaster were comforted?

- What would happen if we had a vision of tolerance that led to connecting and identifying with the common thread of human brokenness shared with people of all color?

- What would it be like to know that race, creed, color, religion or none, and sexual gender and orientation of all types were celebrated equally?

- What if you were hungry and I simply offered the food that I have?

These questions motivate and inspire a vision of tolerance. Whether in church, a Twelve Step group, or a village, tolerance would ask the question, "What kind of community do we want to create?" There is less focus and concern about what is in it for me and more of a consideration of the good of others.

Tolerance does not shrink back in the presence of domination. Dr. Martin Luther King Jr. put it this way: "Darkness cannot drive out darkness; only light can do that. Hate cannot drive out hate;

only love can do that." The energy of tolerance intensifies love and diminishes hate. The only way to harness this energy amidst hate is through the consummate vision of the one who loves.

Openness to Differences

When we are afraid, we close our hearts to others because we fear being hurt. The reality is that sometimes we get hurt by others. When we close our hearts with judgment and isolation, we separate ourselves from the vision of tolerance. By doing so, we promote coldness and penetrating loneliness that divides and ultimately destroys human connection.

Twelve Step meetings embrace being open to differences. When walking into a Twelve Step meeting, it is like saying, "I am not the same as you, but I am connected to you through common struggle and suffering of a shared addictive behavior."

The life of an addict is full of deception, loneliness, and isolation. As addicts, we are driven by a closed view of reality between us and our drug of choice. Inside the room of recovery, there is all the possibility of promise. When we open our heart to differences by embracing likenesses, we become open to diversity.

Cooperation, Not Competition

Earlier, I shared how a competitive spirit can fragment and fracture the spirit of community. Competition definitely promotes improved results with any endeavor. Yet, the nature of competition creates a zero-sum mentality. There must be winners and losers. At a microlevel, those who win are judged as being successful, hard workers, and worthy of reward. Often, those who lose are judged as the opposite. The end result is that those who "have" get more while those who have less "have not." From a macro view, this mentality has created an intolerable gap of disparity and greed.

We cultivate tolerance through cooperative spirit. In a world of greed, cooperation is a necessary ingredient for tolerance to thrive and flourish. This spirit generates ideas and strategies that make our world sustainable.

Acceptance of Those Who Are Different

Being forced out of my comfort zone fuels parochialism and makes it difficult to accept others. It's easy to become narrow minded. When I see the world only through my eyes, I become blind to the different views and experiences of others. I am liable to become locked into a battle for supremacy. It's easy to envision our world as my space versus your space. When we do this, we divide community into "us" versus "them." This dynamic creates distance within community and accelerates intolerance and a lack of acceptance of others.

Starhawk, an American teacher, writer and activist, delineates how power can diminish acceptance and warns against the domination from those who embrace a power-over dynamic. She explains power-over as manipulators trying to get someone to do something against their will. It can take the form of positional power as in the ecclesiastical hierarchy of a church or the military armed forces. The ongoing, tragic crisis of sexual abuse and harassment within the Catholic Church is a clear example of this form of power abuse. Positional power can be taken for granted by those who have it.

Many activist organizations utilize obstructive power. Other forms of power include institutional, cultural, and structural power.

Institutional power activates economic, legal, and political power that is directly wielded by institutions. Cultural power is the cultural norms, conditioning, and privilege regarding race, class, gender, age, and ability from the perspective of the dominant culture. For oppressed people, cultural power is a consciousness of community, class, and culture that serves to empower. Structural power can be covertly exercised within the context of dominant institutions. All of these forms of power can disrupt acceptance of others who are different.

Power over others expresses domination and exclusion, whereas power with others emphasizes the capacity to influence and take action on uniting with others through solidarity, community, and cooperation. This measure of power comes from a vast resource of personal brilliance—your wisdom, knowledge, experience, and skills. Accepting the differences of others supports tolerance and requires using the power with and power within skill set.

It is problematic if not impossible to accept the differences in others if you can't accept your differences. Like many others, addicts engage in a momentous war around self-acceptance. An ongoing wallowing in the mud of past failure promotes self-hatred, undermining self-love and acceptance. This unresolved struggle sabotages the possibility of tolerating others. It also obscures the possibility of making meaningfulness from the ordinary commonplace struggles in everyday experiences.

Listening to the Hearts of Self and Others

We live in a noisy world of voices that pull us in opposite directions. In this digital age of unprecedented technological development, it is more difficult than ever to listen to your heart and the soul of the world around you. There is fierce competition to be heard. Panic often sets in when your thoughts are drowned by a cacophony of voices that overwhelm and inundate through a barrage of tweets and Facebook posts. Sound bites often take the place of contemplative thought and reflection. Yet, when you don't listen to your heart and reflect on the soul and spirit of the world around you, the capacity for tolerance toward others will begin to fade in the presence of narrow-minded bigotry.

By listening to your heart and the heart of someone else, you not only bring peace in the moment but access the wisdom necessary to heal our world. Take time to listen to your heart. Be quiet and let your heart tell you what it needs to say. Write it down and think about it. Listen to whatever your body is trying to tell you about being out of balance. Whether you have a headache or are fatigued, your body is trying to talk to you about self-care. When we are in tune with our bodies, we are in a better position to be in tune with others around us and cultivate tolerance toward them. When we are disconnected and not listening to ourselves and our bodies, it fuels a lack of awareness toward others.

Stress, sadness, anger, depression, and anxiety can be framed as "the voice of God" that we need to listen to. When we listen to our feelings we can determine where we are out of balance. Listening to your feelings allows you to access your inner wisdom and make the necessary adjustments to meet your needs.

When you slow your life down, you cultivate the discipline of listening to your body, emotions, and the world around you. What is the world trying to tell you through body experience and emotional reality? What is your world trying to say to you through your partner, your pets, the birds, the wind, and the whole world around you? You cannot develop tolerance unless you listen to yourself and the world around you. Through listening, we connect heart to heart. There can be no heart connection without listening.

Forgiveness—The Magic Experience of Personal Freedom

To forgive is to set a prisoner free, only to discover that the prisoner was you.

—LEWIS SMEDES

Going deep with forgiveness is always complicated. Growing up with a Christian background, I recall being told to forgive because that is what Jesus would do. If Jesus forgives then you must forgive. For me it wasn't all that easy. First, I am not Jesus. Second, people are not robots who respond to human tragedy with manufactured responses. Forgiveness in the presence of horrific human abuse seems like a mockery.

While catching a ride to the airport, I asked a Somalian man about his background and how he ended up in the United States. He grew up in Mogadishu and during the civil war he and his entire family ran away to hide, but rebels caught up with them and slaughtered his entire family with machetes. He was the only one to escape and survive.

Although I was curious, I thought it would be grossly inappropriate for me to ask this man if he had forgiven those responsible for this horrific crime. We must first embrace feelings of hate, anger, rage, and overwhelming sadness before considering forgiving others. The human condition requires this kind of consideration. You cannot run from hate and rage. You have to embrace it. There is no magic to resolution. You must embrace and feel the experience to move the hate from the person to the issue. That's when you shift the energy from what you hate to what you love. You can only remove rage toward a person by saying, "no more" and then setting boundaries on how to release it in healthy ways.

Forgiveness is a letting-go process. You aren't required to become best friends with the person who has perpetrated the hurt. You are required to let go, or not hold grudges against the person. You allow the healing dynamic of forgiveness to replace the resentment and judgment. When this commitment is made, there is no longer room for throwing up in the face of the perpetrator what they did to hurt you.

Ultimately, forgiveness requires that you identify and embrace how you have offended others in ways similar to how you were offended. By doing so, you can work toward forgiving yourself. This step in the healing process is controversial to those who have been victimized. However, I have never seen victims get beyond the hurt and pain unless they embrace and own how they have victimized others.

I have seen victims of sexual abuse or marital betrayal struggle to embrace their offensive behavior. Egregious victimization can fuel entitlement. My experience is that there is a "victim-victimizer" dynamic in everybody.

Forgiveness requires a demanding skills set. Few enter the forgiveness process without a tremendous internal struggle. The nature of forgiveness augments this response. Forgiveness requires that I embrace and sit with the deepest pain and not medicate it with escape mechanisms. It means I embrace and allow for grief and sorrow to settle in without trying to rush the process with superficial measures. To find forgiveness, it's necessary to go deep into the soul of your heart. You must scrub the wound.

A small child wants his mother to kiss the "owie" when a knee gets scraped from a fall on concrete. The natural response is to avoid scrubbing the wound of emotional hurt, betrayal, and deep pain. Yet, just as the mother knows that it is necessary to clean the wound so it does not get infected, it is necessary to scrub the emotional wound for forgiveness to go deep and heal our emotional selves.

The process of forgiveness can be ugly. I have seen patients who, after hearing a disclosure of infidelity, have vomited, fainted, or released blood-curdling screams because of the painful behaviors perpetrated toward them.

Once the wound is scrubbed, it becomes necessary for the victimized to embrace their offending behavior. We all have one. When facing our offending behavior, as the victimized person, we can work toward the forgiving of self, which simply means, "I will not hold this against myself any longer. I let go."

This process is seldom a "one and done" experience. Rather, we must be willing to go back and reestablish the forgiving of self sometimes throughout the course of a day. The benefit of doing this is that self-forgiveness provides a space for the victim to return to find relief from the emotional prison.

Forgiveness demands courage and bravery to embrace powerful feelings such as hate, rage, shame, sadness, and depression to find the wisdom so necessary to let go of offenses perpetrated by self and others.

Questions

1. Which part of the acronym (VOCAL) about creating tolerance have you struggled with the most:

   a. Vision
   b. Open Heart
   c. Cooperation, Not competition
   d. Acceptance of Other's Differences
   e. Listening.

2. Which part of the forgiveness process do you find most difficult?

3. Who in your life do you need to forgive?

Chapter 9

Going Deep—Allowing Sorrow to Do Its Work

Don't cry because it's over, smile because it happened.

—Dr. Seuss

Sadness and sorrow are two of the most common experiences. For all of us, grieving is average and par for the course. No matter who you are, you will struggle someday with sorrow. Virginia Satir was right when she said, "Life is not the way it is supposed to be. It is the way it is. The way you cope with it is what makes the difference."

Most of us don't do very well with grieving. Uncomfortably, we show tears, wipe them away, and bury the deep loss inside while marching forward into the future. Some don't even show tears; they simply stuff the sadness, become stoic, and appear as if they have it all together. To do otherwise would be considered weak.

For those who want to go deep, sorrow and grief are life-long experiences. Although sorrow is not intended to dominate your life, you must engage loss and grief as part of the emotional landscape that leads to emotional maturity. Life is a tapestry of ups and downs. Success and failure are combined with bitter and sweet and are woven throughout the fabric of all human life. Grief is an experiential education necessary to recognize and better fulfill our personal destiny. How we grieve is as individual as we are.

During early childhood, children whose feelings are not validated do not recognize their emotions when they are triggered. As a result, they become very confused about sorrow and sadness. During early-stage development, a child is most likely spontaneous in their emotional expression. They don't hold anything back. There's a story about a little boy who begged his momma to come sleep with him. His mother tried to console him before leaving the bedroom and mentioned she needed to sleep in her bed with daddy. The little boy responded, "That big sissy!"

These are so many humorous examples of the unabashed spontaneity of children. My sister's six-year-old granddaughter said to her, "Grandma, I know this is going to hurt your feelings, but I think I like the other side of the family better than you." These honest expressions are priceless and leave us way too soon.

Children learn to stuff their feelings, impressions, and thoughts as they get older. While much of this is healthy development around social filtering, what often gets lost in the pressure to learn proper social and family cues surrounding authentic expression of genuine feelings. When kids don't know or aren't being given permission to express feelings like sadness around loss, they become emotionally stymied and carry the sadness of loss from childhood to adulthood. Further, there is a strong likelihood that as adults they will sever the memories that could connect emotional pain to unresolved childhood experiences. They become confused about the prolonged sadness in their lives. As a result, many live adult lives triggered by perplexing unconscious cues that create a chronic, low-grade depression.

Most learn to medicate grief encounters with a cocktail of alcohol and drug abuse, numb out with professional career pursuits, become absorbed in their children's activities or church and social activities, or maybe all of the above. Many don't learn to grieve because they never learned to recognize feelings of sadness and situations that would most likely produce the need to grieve. So many people are stuck and can't go deep with their sorrow.

Four Obstacles to Grieving

Obstacles to grieving include cultural pressure, wanting to escape the pain of grief, and not knowing if or when it will end.

Cultural Pressure

When people face sorrow after someone they know dies, get a divorce, or experience a loss in their professional career, they often feel pressure to get over the grieving and get back to "normal." Throughout my years of counseling those who have lost a mate or a loved one to divorce or death, I consistently hear complaints that friends and family want them to get over the pain and get on with living. I have listened to family members talk in terms of time limits. Mourners of loss feel the strain to put on a smile and perform as if nothing were wrong while hiding the sorrow and saving the grief for when they are alone.

People Who Don't Know Their Own Suffering

People who aren't in touch with their suffering feel awkward around people who are grieving. They think they have to say the right thing. They don't know what to say. It only makes the person who is grieving feel more isolated. Some share that they feel as if they have to take care of the person attempting to comfort them. They feel pressure to tell the comforter that their statement was okay, even though it was a dumbass thing to say.

Often, a wake where friends and family come to pay their respects becomes a social engagement that the mourner absolutely hates. Visitors are laughing and engaging folks they have not seen while the mourner is sad and grieving. This incongruence—chatting with well-doers while dying inside because of loss—is unbearable. Socially, mourners can be put in a space that fosters incongruence and discomfort by being with people who want to wish them the best. To compensate for this, they claim that they are doing fine, when nothing could be further from the truth.

The Pain of Grief

Grief sucks—it's painful and penetrates to the bone. Why not avoid it at all costs? Like so many experiences in life, sorrow is painful and we will do whatever we can to avoid and escape its clutch. We withdraw, get really busy, take Vicodin, drink, obsessively eat, drown ourselves in sexual pursuit, and make a lot of money to avoid the deepest pain that comes with sorrow. Yet, no matter what we do, grief dogs our presence and demands that we address and embrace its experience. Actor Keanu Reeves said, "Grief changes shape but it never ends." Golden Globe winner Michelle Williams said, "Grief is a moving river, it's always changing. I would say in some ways it just gets worse. It's just that the more time that passes, the more you miss someone."

Sorrow creates a stronger bond between people than happiness ever could. Common suffering is a stronger link than common joy. As life unfolds, it is necessary to embrace the process of grieving loss and sorrow. Without deep grieving, we are never present in the here and now. To be present is to grieve well. It is not about being somber and sad all the time. Rather, it's about embracing and expressing sadness with all the intensity of heartfelt emotions. This prevents us from becoming stuck in past experiences.

A couple of years ago, my mother died at the ripe old age of ninety-nine. The day after her death was the first day in my sixty-six years of life without a mom and it sucked! It was helpful to embrace the sadness and allow immediate family and friends to comfort and support me during this time of sorrow and emotional pain.

Not Knowing When the Pain Will End

I cannot predict when the acute pain of grieving will end regarding any particular loss. Some people say they can endure almost any loss if they can just know when the pain will stop. With grief, it is impossible to predict. It is never when I think it will be. My friends are not any better at knowing the end date either.

Sitting with uncertainty is difficult. American novelist and screenwriter John Irving described it this way: "When someone you love dies, and you're not expecting it, you don't lose her all at once; you lose her in pieces over a long time—the way the mail stops coming, and her scent fades from the pillows and even from the clothes in her closet and drawers. Gradually, you accumulate the parts of her that are gone. Just when the day comes—when there's a particular missing part that overwhelms you with the feeling that she's gone, forever—there comes another day, and another specifically missing part."[31]

A friend of mine is a medical doctor and a primary influence in the field of addiction. She lost her beloved daughter to cancer. Prior to and after her daughter's death, I watched from a distance how lost my friend seemed in her grief. She seemed in a fog. She was nowhere near the empowered professional I once knew her to be. She appeared confused at times and languishing in the loss of her loved one. She later confirmed that all of these descriptions were true. There were times I wondered whether she would pull through this difficult sorrow and loss.

She slowly emerged from the tunnel of grief after three to four years and was able to engage with her social and professional world. Today, she moves through her world with more wisdom, poise, and perspective about the meaning of life and suffering. Yet, the truth is she will never be the same. She will never get over the loss of her loved one.

Elisabeth Kübler-Ross wrote, "In reality you will grieve forever. You will not *get over* the loss of a loved one; you will learn to live with it. You will heal and you will rebuild yourself around the loss you have suffered. You will be whole again but never the same. Nor should you be the same nor would you want to."

---

31. John Irving. *A Prayer for Owen Meany.* (New York: HarperCollins, 2012).

How Do I Go Deep with Sorrow?

To go deep with sorrow, you need to embrace your darkness, have the confidence that you'll get back up, and be okay with being vulnerable.

Step 1: Embrace Your Darkness

Only when we know our darkness well can we be present with the darkness of others. Many struggle to embrace sorrow because they have never embraced their own shortcomings and experience of darkness. People who have suffered with their own brokenness due to a loss don't struggle with discomfort while in the presence of another's tragic loss. They have been there. They know that it is not words that are necessary. It's just presence. They are able to be present in the dark moments of another person's sorrow because they have embraced their own. Going deep with sorrow allows this connection. Unless I have gone deep within by embracing my dark times of sadness, loneliness, and despair, I will not connect with those who have done so. Sorrow will remain not just painful but will trigger the desire to escape with measures of avoidance.

Step 2: Generate Unconditional Confidence

To go deep with sorrow, I have to journey down knowing that I can come back up. There is no shortcut. When we feel forced to the edges of life and squeezed, know that if we sit with the fear, sadness, and struggle we will find the confidence necessary to come back up. This step can be intimidating. There are times when hardship and sorrow are so great that surviving them seems impossible. Yet this is how total confidence is created. The

151

confidence comes from comprehending that whatever life brings to us, we will be able to manage it.

Buddhist monk Pema Chodron teaches this concept. She uses the illustration of being in the water on a beach when a huge wave comes in and knocks her over. The power of the ocean rolls her over and over on the bottom, getting dirt and sand pouring through every orifice of her body. Just when she thinks she is going to drown, the wave releases her and she stands up. Then, another wave knocks her down and then another after that. For a while, it seems that this is just the way it is. In time, she learns that though knocked down and rolled, she can survive and get back up.

Confidence comes from being knocked down and getting back up again and again. It is a deep confidence we earn when we embrace sadness, fear, and failure and learn the valuable lesson that we don't control the results of life, only our response to it. Chodron calls this "unconditional confidence." However you describe it, know this peace and surety will require that you embrace your sorrow wherever it takes you. Only then will you have the confidence that you can come back up no matter what you face.

Going deep with sorrow is one of the most difficult experiences for addicts. Early childhood neglect and abandonment set the stage for the imprint of mistaken beliefs about the world. Addicts learn early on when you make mistakes and misfortune happens, there is no coming back up. When faced with the possibility of having to go down to face sorrow, adults addicts rely on their mistaken beliefs about themselves, and their worldview triggers an offensive addiction cycle. This leads to escape and denial and ultimately ends in destructive addictive behavior.

Breaking this pattern requires interrupting the mistaken beliefs and embracing a willingness to go down and experience the fear, loneliness, and sadness of sorrow. It is important to "detox" from the addictive escape and to sit with the emotional pain in the present moment. Practice and conditioning is necessary in a supportive community (most likely Twelve Step). In this manner, an addict can learn to create a new neuropathway in the brain that fosters different behavior and helps the addict develop the capacity to go down in order to come back up. In this way, addicts are able to cultivate peace and serenity and produce the "unconditional confidence" that Chodron describes.

Step 3: Be Okay with Being Vulnerable

In western culture, it is common for men to hide their fear behind machismo. The alpha male is the one most considered to have the confidence that is so coveted to achieve power and position and establish importance. Sports are an excellent example of machoism at its finest. Champions feature revered alpha males who take over and dominate. This image is portrayed as the way for men to achieve manhood.

However, this view of champions demonstrating machismo can easily overlook an important concept of teamwork. There are times within the context of team achievement, the dominant alpha male may need to step back into a lesser role for the greater good of the team. Sometimes super talented athletes never experience a championship in a team sport because in part they fail to recognize the importance of curbing their alpha male dominant mentality for the betterment of the team.

To go deep with sorrow, you need to embrace becoming vulnerable and shed the mask of machismo, or the veil that hides true feelings of fear, sadness, and vulnerability. Former heavyweight champion Mike Tyson had a lot to say about the vulnerability of fear around boxing. He suggested that he never stepped into the ring without a sense of dominating fear. He said, "Fear is the greatest obstacle to learning. But fear is your best friend. Fear is like fire. If you learn to control it, you let it work for you. If you don't learn to control it, it'll destroy you and everything around you. So, one must never allow fear to develop and build up without having control over it, because if you don't you won't be able to achieve your objective or save your life."[32]

Everyone experiences uncontrollable fear in their life at some point. For me, what comes before the act of courage is this "shaky tender" moment. By embracing this moment, I am able go down and face my fear, which creates the deep confidence that I will come back up. No matter what the results are, you can manage and handle it because you have been willing to go down and sit with the undesirable feeling of fear, anxiety, and sorrow.

People go deep when they courageously learn to allow sorrow to do its work. Often, we don't because we fear we will fall apart and not survive the pain that sorrow brings. Yet, whenever someone chooses to embrace their darkness, shed the mask of machismo or the veil that hides true feelings, and go deep with common shared sorrow, they create the genuine confidence that stands the test of time regardless of the results. In this way, we come full circle with sorrow and as Dr. Seuss declared, "Don't cry because it's over, smile because it happened."

---

32. Mike Tyson. *Undisputed Truth.* (New York: Penguin, 2013).

Questions

1. Think and write about a time when you felt sad but felt pressured to hide it because you might be viewed or even criticized as being weak.

2. What are some ways you have avoided the feelings that come from grief? Do you think this was helpful or hurtful?

3. Can you think of a time when you sat with sorrow and it gradually got better? What did you learn about yourself?

4. How has machismo or any other veil to your feelings prevented you from feeling your sorrow?

Chapter 10

Going Deep with the Dread of Obscurity

*It's better for the whole world to know you,
even as a sex star, than never to be known at all.*
—MARILYN MONROE

*I had a book signing where I attracted two people.
One wanted directions to the bathroom and
the other who wanted to buy the desk.*
—ERMA BOMBECK

Obscurity is one of the things that people fear the most. Most of us have either given up or never desired the thought of being a celebrity or famous. Yet, it is part of human DNA to desire to matter and be important to someone. People scramble for professional notoriety and even take classes on how to stand out amidst the crowd. None of this is particularly bad. When I go to workshops or annual conferences, certain people are in all-out pursuit to be noticed. I suspect that this is fueled by the insecurity that comes from a fear of being obscure.

Have you ever greeted a colleague at a conference and noticed she was distracted, looking beyond you to others? You probably questioned your importance, particularly if you were in the middle of your point and she began waving to someone else. Obscurity is a difficult experience. The need to belong and fit in is contrary to obscurity. People fear the loneliness that obscurity can trigger.

With advanced medical care, many people are now living well into their nineties. The dilemma is that when people live that long, they often outlive their capacity to think, as well as their friends and cohorts. The idea of living deep into old age is fearful. It stirs up feelings of loneliness and the fear of obscurity. It is not a comforting thought to end up in a nursing home with people you don't know and who might not ever remember your name because of their or your dementia. Yet, we are challenged to embrace and go deep with the experience of obscurity. Normally, with formidable challenges like aging, we try to not think about it.

Everyone must struggle with this common everyday life dynamic. The melancholy of high school graduation or the ending of an exciting summer camp can trigger some fear of obscurity, thinking that we will never be close to or noticed by these friends again. Any life transition ultimately includes feelings about obscurity.

Not everybody is the life of the party. Many will not even be invited to the party. Ultimately, to be emotionally mature, you need to address the experience of obscurity. Addicts struggle with feeling as if they are on the outside of a bubble looking in. Addicts lament that they never felt like they belonged. To get past the painful experience, they numb out with their drug or behavior of choice.

When I was a college kid, I was pretty immature. I attended a conservative Christian university that put a lot of emphasis on students being born again. At this time in my life, this emphasis was a priority for me. There was this guy, Sigler, who was from Detroit and an outlier. He smoked cigarettes in the dorm and had *Playboy* pinups plastered all over his wall. This was pretty normal for most college guys exploding with testosterone but not here.

A zealous Christian guy from Arkansas was angry that Sigler was not conforming to the expected Christian ethic, and I supported this guy. In a sordid kind of way, I was glad to play tricks on this "heathen." One time, the Arkansas zealot carefully pulled out the tobacco from a cigarette in Sigler's pack of unfiltered Camels and placed a firecracker inside. He then repacked the tobacco, placing the loaded cigarette first in his pack of Camels. When Sigler was standing in line at the Circle K lighting up the cigarette, it blew up in his hand. It was designed to teach him a lesson to not smoke, but more likely it made sport of him.

Students played different "tricks" on Sigler throughout the year to get him to become born again or to at least have fun at his expense. Sigler was a good sport about it, but he didn't return the next year. I have often wondered what it was like for him to be an obscure outlier at this Christian school. Perhaps, I will never know. But there have been many days when I have identified with Sigler, especially after experiencing the loneliness, rejection, and obscurity resulting from my decision to abandon my evangelical roots and forsake the shaming experiences of conservative Christianity.

Today, I am an activist within the context of church, civil rights, and other social organizational change initiatives. I am impressed about the obscure people who have made tremendous differences in these various movements. I have a long-standing experience with the church. I have noticed that the movers and shakers are those who are seriously committed in the trenches of activity, completing necessary and obscure tasks. In the church, the women organized the cottage prayer meetings, made sure the church was neat and organized for a meeting, covered dinners for funerals, and did the heavy lifting in ministries of compassion.

As I study the civil rights movement, I am inspired by the women who behind the scenes made change in this country possible. Women like Ella Baker, Diane Nash, Septima Clark, and many, many more who remain virtually unknown to public history, who courageously risked their very existence to do the behind-the-scenes work so necessary for the ultimate success of the civil rights movement. They labored in obscurity.

In today's fight for migrant rights, there are women who carry the banner of justice, sacrifice their well-being, and work behind the scenes so that disempowered migrants might someday be treated with the dignity and respect of a "legal" human being in a country that identifies them as "illegal."

Growing up and doing the "blue-collar" work of church organizing has helped me to appreciate teamwork. The spirit that I have learned from the women who have influenced me has been: "It doesn't matter who scores the points as long as the team makes the basket." This spirit has been ingrained in me from women like my mother and a host of "unknown women" who sacrificed and lived this motto. Obscurity has been a powerful common thread in the lives of women whose impact will never be forgotten and whose lives have transformed my idea of what making a difference is all about.

No one wants to be forgotten, considered invisible, or unimportant. At the same time, quiet, ambiguous life encounters are critical to the development and growth of individual maturity. Stark moments of absolute esoteric experience is commonplace to us all. Consider how a seed that is planted needs the uneventful interaction with the soil to germinate before the plant bursts forth from the earth's surface and a flower blossoms. The same nurturing applies to character and maturity that results from obscure moments.

The type of silence experienced in obscurity is more inward than outward. It's the place where we sit with life's contradiction and conflict. Most of us have little experience with obscure silence. We hurry past it to whatever is more eventful. But obscure silence is necessary. Obscure moments of silence carry with them a healing property.

Theologians say that 90 percent of Jesus's life—a total of twenty-nine years—was spent in obscurity. This time was no doubt as important as his three active years. This time provided the character foundation for him to endure temptation in the wilderness and the pressure from people all around him. Spending time in obscurity can be difficult but is necessary to build a solid foundation on which you can center; an internal stronghold where you can know and live by your personal and heartfelt values.

Are you ready to go deep with obscurity and discover the unique benefits it provides? If so, keep in mind the following.

Obscurity Is Grinding

Obscurity can be grinding and not feel very inspirational, particularly for an addict. If I choose to see nothing but the dark, I am choosing to have my disease do the looking for me. When I am looking for the extraordinary, I miss the meaningfulness of an obscure moment. To love relentlessly in the small, everyday experiences creates great strength in the average ordinary moments of life. Mother Teresa framed obscurity in everyday acts of love in this way: "Sometimes you think that what you are doing is just a drop in the ocean. But the ocean would be less because of that missing drop."

I recall the certified nursing assistants (CNAs) who cared for my mother and others afflicted with Alzheimer's. The intensity of care they demonstrated day after day in small ways made a big difference to those receiving care. While many of these patients were warehoused and forgotten, these CNAs placed value on the lives of those who feared they would be lost in obscurity. Again, Mother Teresa advocated, "Let us touch the dying, the poor, the lonely and the unwanted according to the graces we have received and let us not be ashamed or slow to do the humble work."

Obscurity Lives Long after We Are Gone

Through obscurity, the investment we make to transform our lives and our culture often manifests in the next generations. So much of who we are depends upon immediate results in the here and now. To create meaningful moments from obscurity, embrace the perspective that the change we hope for will most likely take place in the generations that follow.

Consider the sequoia tree, which takes hundreds of years to mature and develop. So too, the change we hope for in society may take years. Like an old Native American reflection, "You must teach your children that the ground beneath their feet is the ashes of your grandfathers. So that they will respect the land. Tell your children that the earth is rich with the lives of our kin. Teach your children what we have taught our children that the earth is our mother. Whatever befalls the earth befalls the sons of the earth. If men spit upon the ground, they spit upon themselves."[33]

Don't Diminish Your Actions

Refuse to have low expectations about what you are capable of creating. Michelangelo once said, "The greater danger for most of us lies not in setting our aim too high and falling short; but in setting our aim too low, and achieving our mark." Develop a candle flame that burns brightly, regardless of what goes on around you.

Stop Self-Sabotage by Choosing to Believe Deeply in Yourself

Addicts often get stuck in obscure moments with thoughts of self-sabotage. Familiar with chaos and deprivation, addicts often sabotage things when they seem to be going well and in the right direction. Nikos Kazantzakis wrote, "For, by believing passionately in something that still doesn't exist, we create it. The non-existent

---

33. David M. Buerge. *Chief Seattle and the Town That Took His Name: The Change of Worlds for the Native People and Settlers on Puget Sound.* (Seattle, WA: Sasquatch Books, 2017).

is whatever we haven't sufficiently desired."[34] Belief does not have to be dressed with swagger and bluster. The things that are most powerful in life are things you don't see, like the wind, electricity, and belief.

In obscure moments, your belief is anchored in poise and quiet strength allowing you to do the next right thing. Results are the product of sustained expectations. Creating the life you want depends upon passionately believing in what you deem important. Henry David Thoreau remarked, "If one advances confidently in the direction of his dreams, and endeavors to live the life which he has imagined, he will meet with a success unexpected in common hours."

Overcoming self-sabotage is a mark of emotional maturity. Addicts overcome cyclical acting out behavior when they advance with quiet confidence by passionately believing they can create the behavior that they see in their heart.

Don't Let Anyone Define You

Most of the beliefs that dominate our adult experience were cemented in our thoughts when we were vulnerable children. Recognize the mistaken beliefs about yourself and your worldview that were established by what your parents or critical caretakers communicated when you were young and impressionable.

Earlier, I shared when I was in high school I was voted least likely to go to college in a biased poll conducted by a teacher who was upset with me. Later, in college, my advisor told me that I would simply be a typical "nine to fiver," emphasizing that I would be nothing special in my professional career.

---

34. Nikos Kazantzakis. *Report to Greco.* (New York: Gardners Books, 2001).

We are all influenced by comments and attitudes of critical people during impressionable times in our lives. During highly vulnerable and fragile times in your life, if someone important to you called you stupid or lazy, you may have carried that belief with you throughout your adulthood. Addicts carry mistaken beliefs that trigger destructive behavior. By replacing these mistaken beliefs with positive affirmations, you can underscore what you have decided to believe and act upon in your life. This always requires daily disciplined conditioning.

Develop a Mind-Set to Get Out of Your Comfort Zone

In the throes of obscurity, I can bury myself in a routine that reaffirms that I am not capable of becoming all that I am destined to be. In the addiction recovery world, we call this "stinking thinking." Whatever you call it, you can become comfortable and expectant of the results of this kind of thinking and sink into a rut, or your comfort zone. It is important to condition yourself to live outside of your comfort zone.

Consider the story about monkeys in a laboratory that were taught to climb an apparatus and, once at the top, were rewarded with a banana. This was all good until the researchers changed the reward from a banana to a squirt of cold water. The monkeys quickly learned to stop climbing the apparatus.

In time, the researchers added other monkeys to the experiment that attempted to climb the apparatus. Interestingly, the more experienced monkeys would not let the new monkeys climb the apparatus. The more experienced monkeys would pull the newer monkeys down before they reached the top. Eventually, no one climbed the apparatus to get the banana, and no one had to intervene. The monkeys learned to pretend that the apparatus did not exist.

The monkeys' response made me think of how similar it is to an addict's way of thinking. In the obscurity of early childhood, an addict learns that their needs will not be met. Most addicts never got their psychological developmental needs met when they were young children. For them, running up the apparatus to get a banana was the same as reaching out and depending upon an absent parent to be there for them. They experienced abandonment and neglect in the obscure moments of childhood, which was a lot worse than "a squirt of water."

Most addicts learned that they will never get their needs met if they have to depend upon someone else. They learned to reach for something that won't let them down and deliver what it promises. The intensity of the problem increases in that addicts can never get enough of what they really don't want. Therefore, in obscurity, they get stuck doing what doesn't work. Eventually, just like the monkeys, they give up thinking that they can ever get their needs met.

When addicts give up getting their needs met, they feel deprived. Deprivation always fuels entitlement, which is expressed by an "I want what I want when I want it" mentality. By not getting what they need, addicts feel entitled to overcome obscurity by meeting their need through addiction.

In order to shift out of this mind-set, as an addict, you need to get radical in the way you choose to do recovery. This is what going to ninety meetings in ninety days is all about. Addicts committed to getting unstuck will make sure that they radically tell on themselves in meetings, practicing rigorous honesty. They choose to not leave a meeting until they gain one insight to help them stay sober. In addiction, when you find yourself stuck and isolated in obscurity, it becomes imperative that you get outside of your comfort zone and radically seek connection with yourself and others.

Obscure moments in life are places where you can either lose or find yourself. You don't have to prove you are an unrepeatable miracle of the universe. You can create the reality of your dreams by taking one step at a time—by seeing yourself today as the person that you are destined to be. In the end, we can join Trappist monk Thomas Merton in his reflection on obscurity: "Finally I am coming to the conclusion that my highest ambition is to be what I already I am."

Questions

1. Can you think of a time when you were in a social setting and it felt as if the person you were talking to was looking through you to notice someone else? What did the experience of obscurity feel like to you?

2. Did you ever have the experience of feeling like you did not fit in? Describe what that felt like and share with a friend.

3. What is something you really believe in that you think will not be complete in your lifetime and will require future generations to carry the torch toward fulfillment?

Chapter 11

Going Deep by Coming to Terms with Boredom

I think boredom is the beginning of every authentic act . . .
Boredom opens up the space, for new engagements.
Without boredom, no creativity. If you are not bored,
you just stupidly enjoy the situation in which you are.

—SLAVOJ ŽIŽEK

oing deep within yourself always involves tangling with boredom at some point. Most addicts attest to a poor track record of managing boredom. It is one of the dreaded experiences in life that often ends with addictively acting out.

I grew up being steeped with a lot of religion. Actually, I consider the local church I grew up in to be a cult. Cults can be both exciting and boring. Typically, I was forced to attend church twice on Sundays, attend Wednesday night prayer service, and then on another day go "calling" on those who missed the previous Sunday. We went to their home and sort of guilted people for not attending, or at least it seemed this way. Of course, there was a fall and spring revival, which meant I had to go to church every night for two weeks twice a year. This provided for hours of boredom and some experiences that outsiders would think wild and interesting.

My church was described by others as a Holy Roller church. I was taught that people did not understand our faith and we weren't the real Holy Rollers. We reserved that description for people who spoke in tongues, which we did not. But what we did do made up for whatever we didn't do to earn the title of Holy Rollers.

During the congregational singing, there was a lot of emotion. My brother and I would take note to see if Grandma Campbell was well enough to attend the worship. If she was, then there would always be fireworks. Her attendance seemed to spur the music director, identified simply as the song leader, to instruct everyone to turn to page 432, "Amazing Grace." We were to sing all the verses. On the second verse, Grandma Campbell would be cued to "get blessed." This meant that her spirit was in tune with the Holy Spirit, and she would verbally express her joy. What that meant is that she would let out a very high-pitched scream that would literally scare the hell out of you if you sat nearby.

My brother and I learned to time her expression and cover our ears. Everyone else acted as if it were normal. It was just understood that little Grandma Campbell was blessed. Sometimes my Grandma Wells would "get blessed." She would take her hat and twirl it on her index finger while she ran around the perimeter of the church, shouting "Glory to God!"

Then there was T. A. Murphy. During the congregational singing, he would "get blessed." Unlike my grandmothers, his expression took the form of hurdling the pews from the back of the church to the front. If the church was full, people just formed a pathway that allowed him to make his way to the front pew. He would be shouting, "Hallelujah, Jesus is His name" as he hurdled one pew after another until he reached the front and then would go into a "holy dance." Add to that the saints of the church gathering at the altar and everyone praying out loud and you see why we were identified as Holy Rollers. My brother Steve and I were always fearful that one of our friends at school would visit our church and we would be embarrassed.

Revival meetings were designed to save the lost. Our church had two of them a year and the church service would last about two hours. The emphasis was to get people saved so they wouldn't go to hell. We always had contests with teams like "the blues" versus "the reds" to get people to come to the revival services. If your team invited the most people who attended the revival service, then you would win something.

One time, my dad was captain of the red team and the pastor, Brother Gravitt, was the captain of the blue team. The deal was if the red team brought more people to revival than the blue team, then Brother Gravitt would have to crawl inside this doghouse and have his picture taken on all fours. I can't imagine why the excitement, but I remember getting the entire Fryman family (all twenty-two kids) to come to defeat the pastor and put him in the doghouse. It was fun seeing the pastor crawl into the doghouse.

I never did like him, and this kind of felt like payback for all the boring church I had to endure. Of course, this was all for the greater glory of God and his kingdom.

Most of the time we did not have all the ruckus going on during the church service, and it was boring. I had to go early in the morning and sit through a Sunday school class and then endure a long drawn-out worship service of two hours. Then there was youth meeting in the afternoon and the dreaded Sunday night service after that. It turned out to be about five to six hours of church every Sunday. This can be a real bummer for a kid who was really bored.

I practiced all kinds of creative ways to beat the boredom. My brother and I would play basketball by cupping one hand on the back of an empty pew making it in the shape of a basket. One of us would sit at the end of the pew while the other sat halfway down an otherwise empty pew. We would wad up the foil of a Wrigley's gum wrapper and use that for the basketball. We would create an imaginary sixteen-team tournament consisting of the top-rated high school basketball teams in the state of Illinois. We would then play a single elimination tournament.

Each game would end whenever someone reached 20 points. To score, you would have to throw the rolled-up foil into the cupped hand basket with the back of the pew as a backboard. You would have to win by 4 points. That was fun and helpful as it took up a lot of time. One time, when my brother beat me with a bank shot to win the championship, he let out a shout of "*Score!*" which startled the faithful, and my dad made us shut down the tournament. We had to go on to other creative games to make it through the boring church services.

Often, our church conducted tent meetings. They put up a tent on a vacant piece of property, hired an evangelist, and played plenty of barnstorming-type gospel music during the revival service. The same antics in worship often took place during revival tent meetings. The tent meetings would take place every night for two weeks and twice on Sundays. It was murder. I remember trying to pass the time away as a little kid by burying june bugs underneath a pile of sawdust and then waiting to see how long it would take for them to crawl out. The sawdust was used to cover the ground underneath the tent.

Most people did not grow up having to contend with the boredom of a long worship service like I did. Yet, everyone has experienced the need to manage boredom. Maybe it was when you were a kid and you had to visit an aunt or a grandma and sit still and not touch anything. It could have been enduring a long commencement speech for high school graduation in a hot gym with sweat rolling off the end of your nose. Whatever it was, you know the experience.

For the most part, no one teaches us how to effectively deal with boredom. At least, I never got any education on the topic. Typically, you just sit while time stalls and seemingly stops. You wait until the uncomfortable time is over, complain about it, and move on with life. Upon reflection, in the midst of all the traumatic experiences that I have known, I would say that boredom was the most difficult to navigate. I consider my creativity in managing the boredom of church as one of the great innovative exercises in my life.

In retrospect, given the craziness and boredom that I knew as a kid, it is no wonder that addiction became a valid means of coping with and managing my life. The deception is that the relief from addictive acting out is brief, and we just need more and more. As a recovering addict, it is important to become conditioned to tolerate the space of boredom and to creatively make meaningfulness out of it. To accomplish this, I must practice not being titillated or fascinated all the time. Uneventful experiences can moderate the soul and create calm. For this to be true, I must practice being present in the here and now.

Recovering addicts need to establish a comfortable routine about their day. All of the little things matter. Morning rituals are important. The time you get up, hygiene habits, coffee time, breakfast, and contemplation. The way a person structures his day—not too rigid nor too loose—matters. Being accountable for unstructured time will impact the way in which a person manages boredom and addictive thinking. Drawing from childhood creative experience is also helpful when you face the doldrums of boredom. Taking a difficult task that feels dreadful and carving it into doable sections is helpful. Rewarding yourself when you accomplish a targeted goal is a way of adding meaningfulness to an otherwise boring experience.

You can make boring tasks an interesting "game" that helps get through unpleasantry. Consider using the Pokemon Go app. Users testify that the game gets them out of the house. So, let's say you're low on milk. You don't feel like venturing out, but you know that if you don't get the milk, you'll regret it tomorrow morning when you make your coffee. This foresight alone does not motivate you. But if you're playing Pokemon Go, there is an added bonus of catching Pokemon during your excursion.

Another option is to attach rewards to a checklist. For example, after completing Step Four of the Twelve Steps, one person chose to become a sponsor to another person as a way of marking his growth and progress. Others create different types of smaller or larger rewards depending upon the milestone. Linking rewards to a recovery checklist can trigger a dopamine release. Some utilize a pen and paper game of rolling two dice when a task is checked off the list, and whatever the number on the dice shows, you give yourself the corresponding reward.

Unstructured and unaccounted for time is frequently a set up for many addicts to act out. Managing boredom in recovery requires the capacity to sit with dull and tedious moments while utilizing ingenuity and creativity to make meaningful enjoyment from boring experiences with an emphasis upon accountability. Creative game playing is a viable way to address uncomfortable boredom. Boredom is an average, everyday experience.

Questions

1. Can you share an example of a boring experience you endured in your childhood?

2. How have you learned to distract, numb out, and avoid boredom in your life? Is it healthy or hurtful?

Chapter 12

Slowing Down and Creating Solitude

God is the friend of silence.

—Mother Teresa

Slowing down and sitting in solitude can be a scary idea for many. Most addicts I know live a pretty busy life—at least in their head, if not outwardly. Slowing the negative chatter that goes on inside our heads demands that we sit still and lean into the itch of discomfort without scratching. Slowing down often requires embracing the reality of feeling thoughts that are uncomfortable, irritating, annoying, or even menacing. Why would anyone sign up to do that?

Ever since the measure of time, moving through the Industrial Age and beyond, we have quantified life by the clock. We have burgeoned into a culture that has become obsessed with filling up time with endless busyness. Larry Dossey coined the term "time sickness" to describe the obsessive belief that time is getting away, there is not enough of it, and you must pedal faster and faster in order to keep up with it.[35] It has germinated the disease of "more," which rivets the mind with incessant thoughts that we have to do more to keep from being less.

This is a perfect rendezvous in thought that fits most addicts like a glove. Respectively, you can never do enough to keep from being less. This crazed thought pattern becomes the necessary fuel to numb out with the various cocktail of addictions that our mind creates . . . and we create many!

In our culture, there is a race to be the best. The rush to be the best lessens quality control. Accidents all over the world like Chernobyl and the space shuttle Challenger demonstrate that driven rush and fatigue negatively affect quality control. Yet, our culture remains obsessed with doing more and more in less time. At some point, this frenzy demands a sedative for all. The human condition is not capable of living with a tightening scrutiny that squeezes more productivity from every waking second. We're now seeing an uptick in stress-related diseases such as insomnia, hypertension, asthma, and gastrointestinal diseases.

Job stress contributes to untold numbers of Americans missing work. City life increases the pace by ramping up pressure to perform. All this pressure causes people to mistakenly believe that somehow doing more means being more. To survive this rush of

---

35 Larry Dossey. *Space, Time and Medicine.* (Boston, MA: Shambhala,1982).

activity, booster drugs have become popular, even necessary for some. Through the years, I have seen a growing number of professionals who rely upon uppers and downers to get through their fast-paced day. Nursing and pharmaceutical students often fall prey to amphetamines such as Adderall, Ritalin, or Concerta in order to ignore the fatigue and get through their day. Then, they rely upon benzodiazepines such as Xanax, Klonopin, and Valium or alcohol to come down from the high. Opioid use in our country is even more widespread.

To respond to the opioid crisis, we turn to legislation or attempt to crack down on careless physicians or drug dealers. Recently, an Oklahoma judge ruled that drugmaker Johnson & Johnson helped ignite the state's opioid crisis by deceptively marketing painkillers and must pay $572 million to the state. Oklahoma sought $17.5 billion, blaming Johnson & Johnson for fueling the crisis that has claimed the lives of more than 6,000 people in the state. It's the first ruling to hold a pharmaceutical company responsible for one of the worst drug epidemics in American history.[36]

An obvious cost-saving intervention would be to promote slowing down and incorporating solitude into average everyday living. We don't because of the fear of sitting in solitude with anxiety is greater than the fear of a drug crisis sweeping our country in epidemic proportions.

So we rush on. We skim the surface and fail to make real connections with ourselves or others. We lose touch with others in our frenzy, our fear of our emotions, and through our unwillingness to stop numbing it all out.

---

36. Jan Hoffman, *Johnson & Johnson Ordered to Pay $572 Million in Landmark Opioid Trial.* New York Times, Aug. 26, 2019.

Why Is It So Necessary to Slow Down?

The word "slow" has negative connotations just like the word average does. Most of us try to avoid or escape being average. On one hand, we like to fantasize about slowing down. It's nice to reflect what it would be like to have a casual day without work pressures or a to-do list. Yet the reality of this lifestyle is threatening. We fear life slowing down too much.

According to dictionary.com, the word *slow* is defined as "dull, lacking speed about life, struggling to understand, not quick at putting things together." Many of us feel judged if described as slow and uncomfortable about other people's perceptions of us. We want to be thought of as a mover and a doer who gets things done. This seems true even if we fantasize about the desire to be or go slow. So, we tend to remain on the hamster wheel of doing, doing, and more doing.

This flies in the face of the Ecclesiastes writer who reflected that "There is a time for everything." In the sixties, the rock group the Byrds sang the Bible verse about the ongoing changes in life in the song "Turn! Turn! Turn!" There is rhythm to the course of life. There is ebb and flow. There are cycles and seasons. By rushing around, we ignore cycles and seasons. For those in a rush there is one season and it is always defined as putting the pedal to the metal—all out speed.

Most of us don't take the time to think about what we should do to cultivate spiritual and emotional nourishment throughout our day. In *Sabbath*, author Wayne Muller writes, "One of our fears of quiet is that if we stop and listen, we will hear emptiness. If we worry we are not good or whole inside, we will be reluctant to stop and rest, afraid we will find a lurking emptiness, a terrible, aching void with nothing to fill it, as if it will corrode and destroy us like some horrible insatiable monster."[37]

Personal brilliance in spirit is spawned by an unquenchable resilience that unfolds in everyday life experience. By slowing down and embracing feelings that otherwise would have been skimmed or glossed over you cultivate solitude. Think of it like this: When you have an itch that you want to scratch, rather than relieve the itching sensation, choose to steady the course by not scratching. The challenge is to lean into the discomfort and learn that you can sit with the intensity of emotional dissatisfaction.

Sitting with discomfort in a moment of solitude increases awareness and clarifies how best to meet your deepest need. Most of us want to do something—anything to resolve uncertainty. Rather than wait with growing anxiety, we want to get away from the displeasure. We want to disconnect from hurtful feelings that can promote misery. The Tao Te Ching observes, "Do you have the patience to wait till your mud settles and the water is clear? Can you remain unmoving till the right action arises by itself?"[38]

Rushing through life is filled with many pitfalls and dangers, including the fear of emptiness, compassion fatigue, trivializing spiritual practice, and catching the disease of "more."

The Fear of Facing Emptiness

Many people race on with hectic schedules and overwhelm themselves with activity to avoid feeling what might come up if they quieted their souls. This style of living fuels deprivation.

37. Wayne Muller. *Sabbath: Finding Rest, Renewal, and Delight in our Busy Lives.* (New York: Bantam, 2000), 50.

38. Wayne Muller. *Sabbath: Finding Rest, Renewal, and Delight in our Busy Lives.* (New York: Bantam, 2000), 50.

Ultimately, deprivation fosters entitlement to act out with self-absorbed behaviors. The fear of emptiness is at the core of addictive behavior. Writer, speaker, and activist Jean Kilbourne reflected in her book *Can't Buy My Love: How Advertising Changes the Way We Think and Feel* that "addiction begins with the hope that something 'out there' can instantly fill up the emptiness inside."[39]

Addicts will do everything possible to avoid uncomfortable and unwanted feelings. They will always be looking for the next fix. When someone cannot face or embrace how they feel, their capacity to experience intimacy is thwarted. This can be identified as an intimacy disability. Addicts become stuck with emptiness because they do not know how or don't want to embrace who they are or what they feel. Consequently, they are disabled from being able to intimately connect with others.

Once in recovery, there are withdrawal symptoms of boredom and anxiety because feelings that were once numb are now present. Stopping the rush and speed of busyness accelerates the experience of the unwanted emotions. Once an addict seeks recovery and stops acting out, those feelings that were once avoided or numbed reappear. For an addict, slowing down is a threat. Stopping the rush and speed of busyness accelerates the experience of unwanted physical and emotional feelings. Emptiness becomes filled with cravings and the battle of withdrawal begins.

Compassion Fatigue

People who help others can experience compassion fatigue. It is defined as an extreme state of tension and preoccupation toward

---

39. Jean Kilbourne. *Can't Buy My Love: How Advertising Changes the Way We Think and Feel.* (New York: Simon & Schuster, 2000).

the hardship and suffering of others. This focus can create a secondary traumatic stress for the helper. People in helping professions and caretakers in family relationships are vulnerable to compassion fatigue. Often the rush and push of trying to do more in less time triggers not caring for yourself, which has its own trauma. Many caretakers become victims of diseases caused by stress and a lack of self-care.

Trivializing Spiritual Practice

Being in a hurry fuels impatience. In a world of rush, spirituality is reduced to fast-food faith, or thinking of God as a spiritual vending machine. For example, we pray to God for stuff that we think we need. Spirituality is reduced to pragmatic insurance during hard times.

A Disease of "More"

Considering the development of technology designed for efficiency, you would think that eventually you would accomplish enough or accumulate enough stuff. Yet, in our society, a disease of "more" seems to be rampant. According to the National Association of Home Builders, the average size of a new single-family U.S. residence in 1950 was 983 square feet. Today, it is nearly 2500 square feet. As home sizes ballooned over that time, family size shrank. The U.S. Census Bureau reports that in 1950, an average American family consisted of 3.8 people; today's average family contains 2.6 people.

Many of us never seem to have enough money, a big enough house, or enough material possessions to achieve satisfaction. We don't bother to ask the question, "When is it enough? In some ways, it's as if there is a mentality to gather up more and more out of a fear of having less. For some, the drive to achieve, succeed, and accumulate is rooted in a fear of failure, not having enough, and being left out. It is abundance driven by scarcity.

The Purpose of Slow and Solitude

When I drive my car through a neighborhood, invariably I cross into a school zone or through a neighborhood with a cautionary sign that says something like, "Slow, children at play." Immediately, I brake and proceed cautiously attempting to be alert to the possibility of a child darting into the street to cross or chase after a ball. The whole idea of the sign is to create safety for all.

Mentally slowing down is a way to gather my thoughts, faculties, and senses in order to proceed with appropriate caution. It's a way of providing safety for the soul. In the midst of a rushed existence, slowing down to make way for solitude is helpful in grounding and centering the soul. Slowing down and carving out a place in solitude is the way to access your personal brilliance.

Author Thomas Merton in *Conjectures of a Guilty Bystander* wrote, "There is a pervasive form of contemporary violence to which the idealist most easily succumbs: activism and overwork. The rush and pressure of modern life are a form, perhaps the most common form, of its innate violence. To allow oneself to be carried away by a multitude of conflicting concerns, to surrender to too many demands, to commit oneself to too many projects, to want to help everyone in everything, is to succumb to violence. The frenzy of our activism neutralizes our work for peace. It destroys our own inner capacity for peace. It destroys the fruitfulness of our own work, because it kills the root of inner wisdom which makes work fruitful."[40]

In my twenty-five years as a pastor, there were times I clearly succumbed to the frenzy of activity and brought on overwhelm. As a therapist, there are many times I've exhausted myself by thinking of ways to be helpful to others and thinking about content from workshops I've attended. I confess that during those times I truly felt violence in my heart.

It takes some people many years of overwork before they want to take the time to cultivate a place and a sense of solitude in their lives. There are times we think we need the busy, the commotion of activity, and the interaction so we don't feel lonely or empty. Yet, only when we turn inward to lonely and empty are we able to transform them into peace, solitude, and meaningfulness.

When we slow down, we learn to quiet our spirit and face our true selves. It takes a quiet space in my head to know my true self. Long extended times of quietness is the only way to unmask what is superficial in my life. The silence can pop the imaginary bubble we create that makes it seem we are on the outside looking in on others who are happy, connected, and living meaningful lives. It dispels the illusion that everyone is happier or experiencing more joy and peace than we are. Many of us live with this powerful illusion our entire lives. It's not real. By embracing solitude, it's possible to recognize that the average and uneventful is the only environment in which peace and happiness can be born.

When I was a child, I daydreamed about living somewhere other than where I lived. We were sort of poor. There were other

---

40. Thomas Merton. *Conjectures of a Guilty Bystander.* (New York: Doubleday. 1968).

people in our town who were more poverty stricken. But we had twelve kids, and six of them were boys. We always had bare spots in our front and back yards from playing ball. Our wooden front steps were often broken because of the rubber balls we threw against them. In short, I didn't live in a very pretty house.

At Christmastime, I recall riding my bicycle through rich neighborhoods. The homes sported these beautiful full and big Christmas trees in their big picture windows. I thought, *Wow, wouldn't it be nice to live in that house with that family? I'll bet everyone is so happy and excited about Christmas.* Later, as a pastor and therapist, I learned what an illusion that was. Wealthy people from similar neighborhoods shared their stories with me of brokenness, stress, and sadness that belied my illusion. No matter how much money you have or don't have, solitude is necessary to confront the raw and the real and to break through the False Self.

There is a time for everything to exist and to be, so says the Ecclesiastes writer. (Ecclesiastes 3). This speaks to a certain cadence and rhythm about life. There are circles, cycles, and seasons of life that bookend experience and contribute to meaningfulness. When you eliminate these cycles, unravel the circles, and ignore the seasons, you miss what brings insight and meaningfulness to life. The drive for excellent results pushes people out of your circles, cycles, and seasons.

People who don't stop to embrace emptiness in both thought and experience run through life in a hurry attempting to avoid "nothingness." Yet, it's the void of nothing that brings forth the existence of everything. The Tao Te Ching states, "If you want to become full, let yourself be empty. If you want to be full let yourself die."

In emptiness, we learn to let go by embracing our inner conflict and facing uncertainty. For most, this is a painfully enduring process as we face our negative narration about life. Embracing emptiness becomes a process that Henri Nouwen describes as "a place where the old self dies and the new self is born."[41] It is a place to let go of the fearful, hate-filled, and rigid judgments of self and others.

In solitude, we can empty ourselves of prejudices and let go of the idea that one must be right and one must be wrong. It creates a space where our innate brilliance begins to surface naturally. In the practice of embracing emptiness, we can become more attentive to the still small voice of personal brilliance that exists within us all. Solitude promotes the sacred ground of emptiness that is the seat of all things authentic from within. It is life's greatest paradox.

The combination of slow and solitude demands dormancy. Just as the seed needs the dormancy of winter in order to sprout in the spring, our soulfulness needs the dormancy of emptiness to give forth the flower of our personal brilliance. This requires cultivating a certain solitary mind-set through daily ritual.

How Do I Slow Down and Cultivate Solitude?

According to Thomas Merton in *Rhythm of Life*, "Music is pleasing not only because of the sound but because of the silence that is in it: without the alternation of sound and silence, there would be no rhythm. If we strive to be happy by filling in the silences of life

---

41. Henri Nouwen. *"The Way of the Heart."* The Prodigal Catholic Blog. https://richardconlin.wordpress.com/2013/08/09/the-way-of-the-heart-henri-nouwen/.

with sound, productive by turning all life's leisure into work, and real by turning all our being into doing, we will only succeed in producing a hell on earth. If we have not silence, God is not heard in our music. If we have not rest, God does not bless our work. If we twist our lives out of shape in order to fill every corner of them with action and experience, God will seem silently to withdraw from our hearts and leave us empty."[42]

Slowing down and forming a place of solitude is not complicated. However, sometimes, simple things can be very hard to do. When we live in a world of complexity, stress, and drivenness, creating a space for solitude can be a challenge. Being centered and focused demands incorporating a sense of slow within the context of each day and season in life.

I have counseled addicts who are workaholics and drive themselves into exhaustion. To compensate, they medicate by addictive acting out. By not having a ritual of slow time sometime during the day, they create a surefire pathway toward relapse.

Slowing down can be scary for someone who struggles with quietness and solitude. By eliminating the clamor and noise, it is just you with you. Most people do not spend a lot of time with just themselves. Solitude is an experience that beckons all of us to retreat at least for a short time. During solitude, you can get clear about who you are, what you are to do, and where you are to be. When we slow down the pace, we create a shortcut to reaching a goal.

Slow, it turns out, is quicker than multitasking. According to "The Science is Clear: Why Multi-tasking Doesn't Work" the ability to multitask is a myth. The article cites one study that

---

42. Thomas Merton. *No Man Is An Island.* (New York: Houghton Mifflin Harcourt Publishing, Shambhala, 2002).

found just 2.5 percent of people are able to multitask effectively.[43] And when the rest of us attempt to do two complex activities simultaneously, it is simply an illusion. We are unable to do more than one thing at a time. Slow creates presence—the most-effective space in which to be doing the task at hand.

Solitude restores life balance as we create a sense of poise and peace, perspective, and centered living. Solitude creates the capacity for life to come to you rather than you pushing and prying energy to make things happen. Solitude slows your heart so the brilliance that exists within you meets the flow of life moving with you. That's what people mean when they say, "Go with the flow." Solitude encourages us to go with the flow. When this flow of life energy meets your inner brilliance, every day can feel like a miracle.

To embrace the concepts of slow and solitude, you need to feel emotionally safe. To do this, you need to embrace humility, sobriety, and gratitude.

Humility

Humility doesn't need too much space. Arrogance takes up other people's space. Humility helps us decrease so that those who do not have enough space can have more. It requires you to not compare or puff yourself up in consideration to others. Many leaders of professional organizations spend a lot of energy grappling for positions of importance, power, and prestige. Humility eliminates this struggle by leading you to places and people that no one is competing to serve.

---

43. Cynthia Kubu and Andre Machado. The Science is Clear: Why Multitasking Doesn't Work. (Cleveland Clinic, 2017). https://health.clevelandclinic.org/science-clear-multitasking-doesnt-work/

I love the story told by Wayne Muller regarding Henri Nouwen, who had been working with the disabled. Nouwen received a call from the White House to provide special counsel during difficult times. He declined, reasoning that the White House would find someone else to fill that treasured position. He did this because his friend who was disabled would have no one if he chose to leave to go to the White House. With humility, he stayed put. Mother Teresa underscored that we do no great things, only small things with great love. This is who we are and how we find ourselves in a spirit of humility.

Sobriety

Your mind can only slow down and find meaningful solitude through sobriety. You must stop the runaway train going down the track. This includes out-of-control busyness, worry, and addictive acting out. When your mind is distracted and tormented with thoughts and behaviors that medicate discomfort, you can't create solitude. You must slow down and embrace the painful reality your out-of-control behavior has created. By doing so, you create a space for solitude. There can be no meaningful solitude in the absence of sobriety.

Gratitude

Slowing down life's pace and finding a common space for solitude requires embracing gratitude. Gratitude takes what is and makes it more. In *The Language of Letting Go*, author Melody Beattie writes that, "Gratitude unlocks the fullness of life. It turns what we have into enough, and more. It turns denial into acceptance, chaos to order, confusion to clarity. It can turn a meal into a feast, a house into a home, a stranger into a friend."

Gratitude is a necessary component in the development of solitude in your life. It provides the creative juice for truth to arrive in a moment of solitude. It establishes a spirit of safety that harmonizes with slowing down. It is from a space of gratitude that you regain poise and perspective. Gratitude provides the emotional oil to flow with your inner brilliance and cultivate meaningfulness in common experiences of average everyday living.

Solitude is fostered by slowing the pace of life through embracing an intentional reflective life. Mindfulness meditation, guided imageries, and times when you eliminate the distractions in life all cultivate solitude. It's not scratching the itch but sitting with the irritation with a plan of allowing your irritations to yield meaningful wisdom and understanding about yourself and others.

In *Radical Grace*, Richard Rohr states that "the simplest spiritual discipline is some degree of solitude and silence. But it's the hardest, because none of us want to be with someone we don't love. Besides that, we invariably feel bored with ourselves, and all of our loneliness comes to the surface."[44]

Questions

1. Which area of your life suffers the most because of your rushed and hurried life?

   a. Family
   b. Other relationships

---

44. Richard Rohr. *Radical Grace: Daily Meditations.* (Cincinnatti Ohio: St Anthony Messenger Press,1995).

    c. Recreation

    d. Work

    e. Spirituality

    f. Health

2. If you were to sit alone for a significant period of time, what feeling would you most dread addressing?

    a. Loneliness

    b. Depression

    c. Resentment

    d. Anxiety

    e. Shame

    f. Hate

    g. Other

3. Humility embraces the reality of not needing too much space. Where do you tend to demand too much space in your relationships? Reflect upon your various relationships and assess ways in which they become more about you and what you want versus what others want and need.

    a. Professional

    b. Children

    c. Spousal/romantic partner

    d. Family of origin

4. In what ways have you not been sober? How has that sabotaged solitude in your life?

5. How has gratitude taken what is and made it more in your life?

Chapter 13

Stalking the Shame
that Blunts Brilliance

Nobody ever beat themselves up to a better place.
—KEN WELLS

There is no life experience that disconnects us faster from our personal brilliance than shame. At one point or another, we all struggle with shame. It doesn't matter if you are poor, wealthy, famous, or infamous. Shame stalks everybody.

Former major league baseball player Bill Buckner played more than 2,500 games in a career that spanned twenty-two seasons. His career included hitting over .300 seven times with a career batting mark of .289. His longevity and achievement would argue for Hall of Fame consideration. Yet, he is most remembered for the error he made in a crucial World Series game. Perhaps no greater shame and defame has been cast toward any one player's error than Buckner's blunder as a first baseman in the 1986 World Series.

Going into the sixth game, the Red Sox were leading the series three games to two. Catcher Gary Carter, the Mets's last hope, fought off a two-strike pitch for a single, and the Mets regained a spark of hope. Kevin Mitchell followed with a single of his own, and then Ray Knight hit another single to load the bases with two out in the ninth inning.

Mets fans were giddy, hopeful, but still afraid. Their team trailed 5–4 and was one out away from finishing their spectacular season, and one win away from being miraculous. Then, with Mookie Wilson at the plate, Bob Stanley's improbable wild pitch brought Mitchell home. All of a sudden, the Mets and the Red Sox were tied.

The scene is now set for a most improbable ending. With all the drama of a ninth-inning, two-out World Series championship on the line, Wilson chopped a 3–2 pitch up the first baseline, and Buckner, the veteran, positioned himself to field what appeared to be a routine grounder and out. However, when he attempted to field the ball, he missed. It went between his wickets and into shallow right field.

Ray Knight rounded third and head for home, jumping with joy. The Mets had won the game! They tied the series at three games apiece and won a come-from-behind seventh game to become world champions.

Boston fans could not let Buckner's error go. Buckner became the goat, and his name became synonymous with the word "choke." Even though he had a sterling, near Hall of Fame career, for many Red Sox fans he will only be remembered for the error, along with Stanley's wild pitch, that cost the Red Sox game six and the 1986 World Series.

Folklore has it that Buckner struggled with the criticism during the ensuing years. At some point he stalked the shame that hounded him. He eventually confronted the payload of misbelief carried in the shame and separated himself from the dirge of criticism.

Legend has it that one day Buckner ran into Mookie Wilson at a baseball event years later. Apparently, Wilson felt awkward when Buckner connected with him in a friendly way, kidding about Wilson hitting him some ground balls. He wanted to ease the discomfort by jesting because he knew Wilson was uncomfortable about the situation. With class and dignity, Buckner shifted criticism away from Wilson or himself and made light of the error in the present moment. After years of struggle, he demonstrated how he was able to place the shame on the historic error of the past and no longer on himself in the here and now.

Sometimes you make mistakes that you just can't let go of. Maybe you said something hurtful to a loved one. Chances are, as soon as the words got out of your mouth, you wanted to take them back, but you couldn't. Maybe it was something like authorizing a business decision or giving or receiving financial advice. You wish you could erase what happened, but you can't.

Things happen in life that eat at you. You can't sleep it off or drink or eat it away, and time makes it worse, not better. This phenomenon is best described as a shame attack. When shame attacks, it's like being blasted by bear spray or a skunk. You just can't get it off or get away from it. It is like being chased through the woods by a pack of tenacious wolves—they never back off and you keep trying to run—realizing that there is no escape. When experiencing shame, people self-sabotage and are counterproductive.

Often, people say mean things, deprive emotional support and even literally flagellate themselves when they make mistakes. Mercilessly, they offer no self-forgiveness. This response is projected toward others with criticism and judgment. It becomes a wicked vortex that Alice Miller refers to as "soul murder" in her book, *For Your Own Good: Hidden Cruelty in Child-Rearing and the Roots of Violence.*

When I played basketball in the seventh grade, I was pretty good. Good enough to make the team and even to be one of the starters. Yet, when I played and made a mistake, I would scream at myself and run up and down the court. This proved to be counterproductive. Paralyzed by one mistake, I set myself up to make another and then another mistake. Once, my coach yelled at me: "Wells, get your head out of your ass!"

I never did. Soon, I was on the bench sitting next to the coach while someone else played my position throughout the season. Many years later, I understood that nobody ever beat themselves up to a better place. Away from the scrutiny of my coach and the pressure I put on myself in game situations, I became a great practice player. I never learned as a kid to manage the shame of making a mistake. I never found an alternative to self-criticism. It took years into my adulthood before I figured this one out.

Likely, the most profound lesson that an addict must learn is that you cannot beat yourself up to a better place. Addicts who have relapsed confess to me that they feel dominated by shame. They can't believe they made the same mistake yet again. They suffer despair and hopelessness. Some have even committed suicide because they cannot stop berating and beating themselves up. Death seemed better than this continual beating up of self.

Addicts in recovery with long-term sobriety must learn to stop beating themselves up because of a mistake. Instead, they need to forgive themselves. Rather than wallow in the mud of failure, it is necessary to embrace the vision of the person you desire to be and walk "as if" you are that person. This is what destiny asks of every person. You need to see yourself as an unrepeatable miracle of the universe.

Addicts who suffer chronic relapse have failed to utilize this critical recovery tool. Self-forgiveness is about relating the guilt and choosing to no longer hold the acting out behavior that you committed against yourself. It's forgiven. This isn't about giving yourself a pass from the responsibility of the behavior you committed. Rather than lamenting with negative self-talk and relentless criticism, embrace bringing yourself back to center where you'll find sobriety and peace.

Long-term sobriety is absolutely dependent upon being unconditionally gentle with yourself while remaining adamant about doing whatever is necessary to stop acting out. Whenever you beat yourself up, you are increasing the probability and likelihood of relapse.

The Role of Velvet Steel

Throughout my recovery from addiction, I have learned to practice Velvet Steel in my personal life, and I routinely teach addicts this extremely important skill. Velvet Steel is the practice of applying gentleness where velvet (gentleness) is needed and steel (toughness) where steel is required. This is not an easy skill set to master, but is absolutely necessary for solid recovery.

A common pattern for addicts is to be tough on themselves when they need to be gentle and gentle when they need to be tough. They tend to get the dynamic turned around. Being tough should involve an action plan and a willingness to do whatever it takes to remain sober in the presence of a craving.

As addicts, the biggest challenge, the one that causes the most struggle, is relapse. During the earliest days of my recovery, sobriety was difficult to maintain. I tended to be a perfectionist. Knowing what I needed to do and then feeling powerless to do it triggered much shame in my life. Wallowing in the mud of failure only produced more failure. It was only when I learned to discipline myself to ignore the voices that screamed *you are a screw-up* and *you will never get it right* that I learned to be gentle with myself and bring myself back to center, which is a place of sobriety.

After doing this long enough, I eventually learned to separate addictive acting out behavior from who I was as a person. This takes ongoing practice, with only incremental gains toward mastery. Most of us will be working to improve this skill set for the rest of our lives. To manage shame effectively, we have to condition and train ourself as we would train to run a marathon. But it's worth our time.

Moving away from familiar, self-destructive behavior is difficult because the tendency is to act out how you feel about yourself. Often, people allow their feelings to dictate how they respond to a situation. To practice Velvet Steel, it's important to work through feelings that undermine and trigger mistaken beliefs and learn to act according to what you are committed to believing about yourself, not how you feel. This is where the private personal struggle ensues. You must condition yourself to overcome this difficulty.

Learn to practice unconditional friendliness toward yourself even when you make a mistake and act out. For many, this is foreign concept. Shamed-filled messages that are deeply etched into your personal view dictate that you condemn and criticize your behavior. Shame comes from many sources. Those of us who grew up with fundamental religious teachings may struggle with shame induced by the theology of a condemning God. Many others struggle with shame from negative messages from our parents and caregivers either verbally or nonverbally.

At its core, managing shame requires determining what it means to live a centered life according to your values. When I live a centered life, I am most likely to be congruent, which suggests that my words and actions promote those values. When I don't live a centered life, my values are not in harmony with my feelings, my statements, or my actions. Incongruity fuels shame while centered-living diminishes shame. Being accountable to someone who will hold your feet to the fire when you are off will help you achieve that balance.

To avoid self-induced criticism, we have to learn to stay the course. When we veer to the left or right of center, we can practice bringing ourselves back to center. This process is likened to training a dog to not chase the neighbor's cat. With discipline and repetition, the dog learns to "stay" upon command, only because of the conditioning. That's how we overcome the tendency to beat ourself up. We are gentle on ourself instead of tough. Velvet Steel.

This is the mundane, average space all of us must face. When you face this struggle, you shift out of shame and anchor yourself in your personal brilliance. To do this, you must quietly grow in your capacity to practice Velvet Steel.

Be Your Own Guru

Toxic shame is paralyzing and triggers the loss of selfhood. Shame breeds shame. Addicts believe that no one could love them and therefore, they cannot love themselves. It gives birth to the belief that "I'll be okay—I'll be normal if I can just act out." That's why we feel so uncomfortable in our own skin. It's as if all these other people—but not you—are good and doing the right things but you cannot truly relate to them. To compensate, you attempt to be just nice and polite around them. After leaving, you go get plastered, high, or fuck your brains out with someone to soothe the unbearable discomfort.

Shame can turn people into a human doing rather than a human being. When shame dominates, your sense of worth is always determined by the outside, never on the inside. So, people tend to look to others around them and feed off their accomplishments and build others into personal gurus by putting their achievement on a pedestal, even living through their lives. The reality is that others (including gurus) struggle with the same shame we all share. Shame is a common thread as we all engage through our common brokenness. We look to others because it is a way of avoiding us and our shame.

So, when shame stalks you like a pack of wolves chasing you through the woods, it is necessary to stop, turn around, and face the gnashing teeth and menacing growls of the wolf pack. When you do, astonishingly, you discover that pushing through the feeling of shame is comparable to penetrating paper-mâché. There's nothing of substance to it on the other side! This is what I call stalking shame.

Pema Chodron offers excellent concrete, practical advice regarding steps toward cultivating unconditional confidence in her book entitled *Unconditional Confidence: Instructions for Meeting Any Experience with Trust and Courage*. Regarding stalking shame, her advice is you must be willing to engage discomfort. Shame is uncomfortable. Leaning into the discomfort of shame requires that you embrace the reality of the painful feeling until it becomes unbearable. At this point, you must believe that going down will bring you back up. When you feel the pain, darkness of depression, the despair of loneliness, or the ashen taste of failure, sitting with the discomfort yields the capacity to come back up. Sitting with discomfort cultivates resiliency. It may feel intolerable or as if we will die by doing this, but we don't.

Some people believe that "God will not allow me to go through more than I can handle." I have learned this not to be true. When pain is overwhelmingly triggered and mired in complex trauma, you will need outside professional support. Ultimately, the goal is to help you become your own guru, with or without the assistance of therapeutic or pharmacological intervention.

As you become your own resource, you learn to create a mix of outside support to face the illness and pain that exists on the inside. You learn to live in consultation rather than exist in isolation. The unconditional confidence that rises from facing the dynamic of shame is not about having control over the end result; rather, it stems from resiliency. It is the confidence that whatever the result, somehow you will face it and transform shame into something meaningful.

Realize that no one embraces shame without fear. You may be quaking, jittery, or even trembling with terror and anxiety. No one avoids this experience when addressing the dynamic of shame. It is possible to experience fear and still stalk shame.

Stalking Shame in Six Steps

The following are practical, self-empowering steps to take when attempting to stalk shame.

Step 1—Recognize the Nature of Shame

Researchers have penned volumes regarding the nature of shame. Basically, toxic shame is a powerful dynamic that tells you that you are not okay. It is not just your action that is not okay; you are not okay as a person. Shame creates an internal rupture that produces self-condemnation and a desire to pretend that you are not who you really are. Shame separates you from your authentic, genuine self. Personally, I don't know of anyone who does not struggle with shame. The question isn't how to get rid of all the shame but how to reduce and manage whatever is there.

I liken shame to acid in a car battery. If you keep the acid in the battery, it will help you start your car every morning. However, if you allow the acid to come into contact with your skin, it will burn you. Shame is this way. If you allow shame to come into contact with your personhood (which is who you are), it scars and mars. However, if you direct the shame to its source, it can power empathy and compassion. There are two primary sources of shame: historical (often a childhood experience) and shameful behavior.

First, recognizing you have committed shameful behavior indicates you do not suffer a more serious psychological illness that would prevent you from even caring that you did. Separating the hurtful behavior from yourself is absolutely necessary in managing toxic shame. Candidly, it is possible to commit "shitty" behavior without being a "shit." When this powerful distinction is not made, you get stuck in toxic shame, which generally creates more shameful behavior.

Shame has a vortex nature to it. To manage and shift out of this vortex of thought takes conditioning and training. Addicts, particularly, must rehearse that acting out is an aberration of who they are; it's not their identity. To identify yourself as an alcoholic or other addict has to do with the destructive behavior—not the nature of who you are. Behavior, positive or negative, never defines who you are as a person. As you practice sifting and sorting behavior from personhood, you mature in this conditioning and learn to manage toxic shame.

Step 2—Recognize the Presence of Shame

Shame often appears in camouflage and is covertly operative. For example, it can be present in approval-seeking behaviors. To the extreme, trying to be more to keep from being less can be a shame operative. There can be a desire to always look good or never get caught with your pants down—to avoid being "em-bare-assed."

Highly functional people can be caught in the vortex of shame through compulsive achievement, as in workaholism. I refer to this as high-side shame. At the other extreme, there is low-side shame, which often paralyzes, leaving a person hopelessly wallowing in self-destructive behaviors.

The experience of shame may be hidden in anger/rage response, sadness/depression, panic, frenetic activity, chuckle/laughter, acts of self-sabotage, resentments, hate, boredom, and more. It can even show up as pain almost anywhere in your body—chest, stomach, legs, neck, shoulders, jaw. The key is to recognize its presence. If you don't, you won't be able to do anything about it.

Helpful tools for dealing with shame include mindfulness meditation, journaling about feelings, and sharing your feelings with others. Somatic experience is a professional therapeutic modality that has proven invaluable in shame recognition. Childhood traumatic experience is often met by splitting off from feelings, particularly shame. Recognizing shame in these situations will likely require therapeutic help.

Step 3—Identify Shame's Message

Look at your emotional reaction to shame. It is common to take something personally when someone does or says something to you that triggers shameful feelings. Shame carries profound core mistaken beliefs that oftentimes come from historical experiences—even ones we may have completely forgotten about.

For example, someone might say, "I cannot believe you did that!" You might internalize the mistaken belief that "you are not enough" or "you don't measure up," even though that wasn't the person's intended message. In the midst of an emotional interchange, you may struggle even to realize the message of shame that you are reacting to. To cultivate this skill of looking for the message of shame, anchor your response in your adult self. Avoid allowing the child within to have the reins of expression.

I often liken reactivity and immaturity that surfaces in an adult conflict like a scene from a western movie on television that I watched when I was a kid. There is this scene that depicts a stagecoach with a team of horses running out of control headed for a narrow passageway bordering a canyon with a 100 foot drop. In the scene, the veteran stagecoach operator, gives the reins to a young boy sitting next to the operator who is hanging on to the side rail with a death grip so as to not fall off. The veteran says to the kid, "Here, kid you are on your own." Now, we all know as long as the kid has the reigns, the stagecoach will end up a the bottom of the canyon. Yet, in the scene, the veteran takes the reins back from the boy, with firmness and confidence. He doesn't kick the boy off the coach because of incompetence. Rather, he pulls the child close to him and he takes charge and whispers into the boys ear, "I know exactly how to get this team of horses under control. I have been here many times before. I can get this team of horses to completely stop and we will navigate this difficult narrow passageway and we all will be safe and sound." And that is exactly what happens. When it comes to stalking the message of shame, you must anchor yourself in your adult self and not allow the child within to take the reins.

As a therapist, I often referee a couple's disagreement in a therapy session whereby the two adults have regressed to two four-year-olds fighting. Identifying the message of shame requires slowing down and maybe even taking a time out to reflect on the message. An excellent resource to help identify the shameful messages you are telling yourself is the communications program, *Core Communication: Skills and Processes* by Sherod Miller and Phyllis A. Miller.

Step 4—Identify the Voice

Once you identify the message, it's important to recognize the voice you hear. When I tell this to patients, they often quickly retort, "Well, it is my voice." While this may be true, we have learned this message from someone. Likely, but not always, it is from your family of origin—Mom or Dad. This is not an exercise designed to assign blame. The idea is to gain clarity about where the mistaken belief originated so that you can become responsible for it. If you don't know where it came from, you will be less likely to know what to do with it.

Step 5—Give the Shame Back and Put the Shame on the Behavior

Once you pinpoint the experience of shame, identify its message, and recognize its source, it's time to give it back and assign it to the hurtful behavior. A number of experiential rituals can be helpful in giving back the shame message to its original source. Emotion-focused letter writing, empty chair conversation, and anger expressive work with a tennis racket are only a few examples of many useful tools to give back the shame to the point of origination.

When the source is a parent, many people are hesitant, fearing that if they do that they will incur a negative response or hurt them unnecessarily. To these concerns, I suggest that you first focus on your reluctance separate from your parents, without them present. Shame will tell you that it is not okay to be angry with your parents or to consider the message they gave you as a hurtful one, whether they intended to or not. Shame will tell you that you do not have a right to confront them about what hurts.

You will have to stalk this message and practice giving your parents the shame in the presence of reluctance—while they are not in your presence. I often hear the question, "Do I have to tell them about the shameful message?" The answer is "no." If this were required, those who have deceased parents would be stuck in their shame. That being said, I do suggest that you explore pursuing a face-to-face sharing with your parents. Often, this exercise is most helpful and healing with the guidance of a therapist. It's just not always required.

It is critical that you prevent the experience of shame from settling into your personhood. Recall the nature of shame being likened to acid in the battery. When shame is allowed to infect personhood, it becomes pandemic to your entire outlook in life. Keeping shame off your personhood requires that you direct shame to the hurtful behavior committed by you or toward you by others. Consider the shameful behavior as an aberration and not as a property that defines who you are.

Rejecting shame takes willful practice and conditioning for the rest of your life. When you do this, a beautiful transformation occurs that exposes the brilliance of your human spirit. Focusing the shame on the hurtful behavior has great healing potential. It converts the shame into a resource of empathy and compassion.

As you ponder the impact of your hurtful behavior on another or the back story of the hurtful behavior that someone has projected toward you, it enables you to shift your energies from shame to care and compassion toward those damaged by shame. Regarding addictive behavior, this transformation from shame to compassion is one of the most healing interventions utilized in treatment.

Exercises that help cultivate compassion toward self and others include impact letters written by offended parties to those who committed hurtful behavior. These letters detail what it felt like to be hurt. Typically, addictive acting out behaviors are traumatizing to people addicts care most about. They are also traumatizing to the addict as well. This reality is often overlooked.

Step 6—Cultivate and Act on Your Vision of Your Destiny

Once we give back the shame to its original source or direct it to the behavior and keep it off personhood, there remains this menacing voice that keeps muttering and moaning with the same negative shameful message. We must manage this inner voice dynamic.

In the movie *A Beautiful Mind*, the actor playing John Nash, a Nobel Laureate in Economic Sciences, declares that he can receive the Nobel Prize award because he has learned to ignore the voices. Schizophrenics are not the only people who hear voices. At times, everyone hears negative voices in their heads. To render the voices inoperative, you must practice ignoring them.[45]

Liken it to the college basketball player who stands on the free-throw line. He is from the visiting team. With no time left on the clock and his team down by one point, he's given two free throws. He makes the first one and his team ties. He makes the second one and his team wins.

---

45. Nasar, Sylvia. *A Beautiful Mind*. (New York: Simon & Schuster, 2011).

While the home-team kids in the bleachers behind the goal are saying everything negative they can about his mother, and making every gesture known under the sun to get him to miss the free throw, the player must dial in and focus. How does he do this? He does it through his previous training. He utilizes the thousands of free throws he practiced in lonely gyms by himself during the summer. Then, he runs wind sprints until he wants to drop and then he shoots the free throws while his teammates are screaming at him.

All this preparation is necessary as the player steps to the line at this critical time. Now he is prepared to face this pressure-packed experience. You can do the same to manage shame in the presence of negative voices.

To be successful, create a list of affirmations in which you will consistently bathe yourself. It becomes a practice in mental hygiene. People in recovery from addiction or other destructive behaviors who do this can transform their belief system and learn to stalk shame rather than be dominated by its message. The key is to embrace an affirmation that you want to be true about your life and, in the moment of weakness, act on that affirmation "as if" it were true in the here and now. As you do this, you make it so.

Belief is an Anglo-Saxon word that means "to live in accordance with." It doesn't mean to feel in accordance with. Yet, when we act out a certain belief, in due time our feelings begin to reflect that action. Many addicts miss out on long-term sobriety and serenity by not dedicating themselves to this practice of cultivating affirmations. Affirmations help us stalk the shame in the average commonplace experiences. In the doing, we uncover the personal brilliance that lies deep within.

Addicts are some of the most brilliant people I know. Their brilliance is a result of the shame stalked in their personal struggle with addiction. To those who have embraced the shame that taunts in the presence of addiction recovery, I share this poem:

Stalking the Lion King

There's a lion and when he roars he's telling me I ain't no
    good—
It's not just what I could but he's bitching what I should.

Every day I look at the struggle I experience in every way—
the shame of the game that drives me insane
the sin- the stain—the emotional pain
a place where the guile and the denial of addiction flow like the
    river Nile—

I try to find the strength to say what I think—
to admit where I have been and say it straight—
there's nothing left about me —
that once you know—
your only response is going to be hate—

Simba stalks me and reminds I can never measure up
Seems useless to try, do program, be true blue—I just want to
    give up—
My mind dances 'cross the horizon of thought,
A.D.D races on and on and drives me to absolute distraught

Stalking the Shame that Blunts Brilliance

I look into your eyes and see the hurt—
the disgust of betrayal
that incredulous sense—
that what was just told can't possibly be real

Innocent trust is gone—an irretrievable loss
Safety—warm embrace—are gone like clouds in my coffee
Triggered by double cross
Shame and blame seem to be my one constant friend
Agony, torture—gut wrenching torment—
you'd think I'd never do it again—

Intrigue is a drunken dreamland—with bewitching charm—
It fades connection—
pushes peace so far away—
Ecstasy eats at reality—
Undaunted enchantment numbs with empty possibility
Playing charades all over again—
drags me back to where I started my day.

Like a hard-nosed hound, the lion never ends its chase
It lures me to the dance, as I look to hide my face
The monkey's talkin' trash in his deep clear voice
He talks about a paralyzed paradise—I quickly lose my choice

I scream in remorse with self condemnation
It seems to matter little
the junkie inside rules craving total resignation

I do it again and again, proving I'm dead inside
I look at your red rimmed eyes and wonder why haven't I cried
But, the lion is roaring though every time he's lied.

Shame's a game that gets played in your head
The chatterbox of blame in the end wishes you were dead
It's acid that bleaches out what should be instead

People wanna say you're a Miracle of God
With scoff and scorn, the lion barks- you've always been flawed
The Monkey is master- powerfully Jones will always prod
He's the sham that beats u down—
belittles and prompts that you're the clown

In darkness the lion is prowling
In silence he dominates—yet, who would ever know
Inside, he's paper tiger with only smack and blow—
Paper tiger promises—like a legless fox who has never walked—
'Cause Nothing ever matters—if the lion is never stalked.

—KEN WELLS

Questions

1. Can you think of a life experience that triggered shame that
   was difficult to let go of? How did it impact you and what was
   the result?

2. Can you think of behaviors that you would like to change
   where you were velvet (gentle) with yourself where you

needed to be tough (steel) or steel (tough) on yourself where you needed to be velvet (gentle)?

3. What affirmation are you willing to commit to telling yourself on a consistent basis?

For example:
- "I am an unrepeatable miracle of the universe."
- "I can take something meaningful from each mistake I have made and let go of the rest and fulfill my destiny."

Epilogue

*Beneath the surface of the protective parts of
trauma survivors there exists an undamaged essence,
a Self that is confident, curious, and calm, a Self that
has been sheltered from destruction by the various
protectors that have emerged in their efforts to ensure
survival. Once those protectors trust that it is safe
to separate, the Self will spontaneously emerge, and
the parts can be enlisted in the healing process.*
—Bessel A. van der Kolk

When my mother died a few years ago at the age of ninety-nine, I returned to my hometown to honor her life. I knew this meant I would need to stalk the shame that dominated my life for so many years. I was going home not only to memorialize the mother I loved. This visit represented a significant opportunity for me to deepen resolution from the trauma of growing up in a dysfunctional family controlled by a religious cult. By doing so, I could stalk the shame that had dominated me and my family for many years. My hope was to give my children a new legacy free from the shame that binds.

With an entourage of family and two dear friends, I began my pilgrimage of shame stalking. I visited my mother's childhood home, where she accidentally burned her sister to death, both playing with candle fire at the age of nine and six, respectively. This experience of shame drove my mother till the day she died to prove her worth by doing loving deeds toward others. I read Maya Angelou's poem, "I know Why the Caged Bird Sings," symbolically releasing my mother from the shame that bound her throughout her life.

I then travelled to the church that had its cult grip on my family. I pointed out to my family and friends the room where I was sexually molested by a pastor who was never held accountable. There, I read a poem that I wrote entitled, "The Indispensable, Invisible You."

Next on the list was the baseball park where my mother, older brothers, and I had played during the critical formative years of my life. It was the place I was told I would never be good enough. In the presence of supportive family and friends, I read my poem about shame, "Stalking the Lion King."

The next stop was my childhood home, where abuse abounded and the seed of sexual addiction was planted in me. With an entourage of support, I read another poem I wrote: "My Experience with a Junkie Worm" and then concluded with a visit to the historic Illinois Central Station.

The train station is a historic site located along the trail of African Americans who fled the South during my childhood in search of freedom from the shame placed upon them. As a young boy, I would walk the rails seeking relief from family and church abuse. Countless thousands of African Americans sought freedom from the shame that bound them to being second-class citizens and worse by way of the Great Migration. At the train station I read another self-scribed poem, "The Dance We've Always Ever Done."

(Note: I've included all these poems in the Appendix that follows.)

I then travelled to my mother's memorial, celebrating her life and struggle.

Adverse childhood experiences are commonplace. Those who dare to courageously embrace the struggle of average everyday adversity and hardship discover the stepping-stones to their personal brilliance.

Appendix

My Experience with the Junkie Worm

I may know days of sanity—
sealed with deep commitment to sobriety
I may long for something richer
that which is deeper more satisfying than sobriety
which melts together life's contradictions and complexities
in the presence of confusion and uncertainty
Perhaps, I will know but for a brief fleeting moment the sweet
song of serenity—
that elusive, evasive intangible described as heaven on earth for
but a few seconds takes me away from deficiency and dearth
Yet, the silk of life experience and the ilk of family heredity
tells me there's something different- something missing in my
pedigree-
Hell is the reality—not heaven-which is but a lie, like Santa
Claus and fairytale
The monkey's off my back but the circus plays on and is Holy
Grail,
I run as hard as I can trying to escape the wolves that chase me
through the wood

No matter what I say about who I am or why I do what I do, I'm
    never understood
Lonely booking is as good as it gets—
the shameover reminds the one who forgets-
My roots were born and have grown in the soil of struggle
My DNA betrayed by craving and binging—my steady constant
    slime
Not getting enough of what I really don't want has been my
    changeless storylinewith
carnage of heart and wreckage all about—
the junkie worm, with con and cajole—tells me 'there's magic
    just one more time'—
With whip and whimper-darkness and defeat takes its toll
there's no magic, no mojo that I can find—
With all the meaning of life squeezed out emptiness
resides with no escape route—
Compassion is love birthed inside before it makes its way out
It grows in struggle, in a heart that knows trouble.
Anger and hate are common bedfellows
they're friends who nag and rag and never let go—
Religion and snake oil salesmen sell sedatives—promising to
    heal
Yet anger and hate remain embedded, an experience to feel-
When I face what I fear and embrace what I feel
I transform my insides—the rage and hate to something that
    is real
It's been the only thing I know that has sustained sobriety
    and transformed a lot of hell into a little bit of serenity.

Appendix

The Indispensable, Invisible You

Power over you is luring, seductive with intoxication
Invisibility is scary-shrouded in isolation.

Do I need to do something to be somebody
Can I dream that everybody can be anybody—

Ahh! There she Stands—splendid, sensual and seductive—
Taking up her space—
Though others say she has no place—

With pride and power—she swings and swaggers her
   sexuality—
Like the reborn caterpillar—her wings of freedom show off her
   radiant soul with hard fought congruency—

How could this be? someone scream in fear—
You're so different—you freak!
You must be queer
Somebody do something—Just make her disappear—
   Please don't make me look into the eyes of her face—
I don't want to see her tears—
How can she do what she did and not be a disgrace
Would someone please, please just erase her face—

Alone at night she walks the streets in agony's crucible
In wretched vexation she knows she's invisible
Wondering in the wee hour of the night 'why is hate so
   indispensable?

DARE TO BE AVERAGE

Does she need to do something to be somebody
Can she dream that everybody can be anybody—

In quiet contemplation she knows you want her dead—
So she walks with invisibility, her heart full of dread—

To hell with teamwork and its downward mobility
Let saints be meek- let them have all the humility
Like the great northern lights- I want to be seen! I demand
   visibility!
Give me power, fortune and fame
I need upward mobility—

Nameless invisibility is like being a worm

If destiny and fate bid that I must be a crawling creature
Then please dear God at least make me a 'Special worm'

Do I need to do something to be somebody
Can I dream that everybody could be somebody?

I celebrate the turn around that leads to taking up less space
the transformation of loneliness to a solitude place.

People say you must network, market to get votes—
Hang out with successful people—learn the ropes.

Whatever I do—does it have to be judged?
Condemned or necessarily deemed as wrong
Can I simply be different with a new kind of song?

Appendix

Can I make peace with my own dispensability?
Can I force importance in the presence of invisibility?

If you think I'm lazy, does it make me inferior?
If you get rich because you work hard, does it make you
    superior?

Is it OK to travel a different road?
Than what I've been shown or anything I've ever been told?

Can I find my dignity
and face the fear of invisibility?

Do I need to do something to be somebody
Can I dream that everybody can be anybody?

Acknowledgments

I want to thank the energy of the universe that faithfully awakened me in the early hours of each morning with the intensity to complete this project. For this, I am truly grateful. Much appreciation and gratitude to my editor, Corrine Casanova, whose guidance was always helpful and much needed. I want to thank my copy editor, Karen Chernyaev; Gabe Cox, project manager; Jody Henning, cover designer; and Andrea Reader, book designer; for their guidance and input. They were a pleasure to work with.

I would be remiss if I did not share my love of and gratitude for my wife, Eileen, who has been a quiet inspiration for me throughout this project and every project I have ever undertaken in our forty-four years together. Finally, I want to thank every average, commonplace person and mundane experience I have ever known.

Ken Wells,
MDiv, MA, LPC, CSAT-S, LISAC

About the Author

A s a senior therapist at Psychological Counseling Services, Ken Wells has twenty-seven years of experience in treating sexual addiction and sex offender behavior. He specializes in confronting denial in addiction and treating the nuance of impact around sex offender behavior. With experience at all levels of providing family treatment around the impact of addiction, Mr. Wells conducts workshops on sexual addiction, shame reduction, and spirituality. Mr. Wells holds a master of divinity from Nazarene Theological Seminary and has twenty-three years of pastoral ministry experience. He earned a master of arts in counseling from Ottawa University and is certified as a professional counselor, a sex addictions counselor, and a substance abuse counselor.

Mr. Wells's previously published works include the *Clarification Workbook*, as well as contributions to several professional journals, including the *Sexual Addiction & Compulsivity Journal*, and three books. An experienced professional communicator, he has been invited to speak on numerous radio and television programs and at workshops and conferences internationally.

Mr. Wells facilitates five men's group with more than sixty-five men focusing on sexual addiction. He was a charter board member of Interfaith Sexual Trauma Institute (ISTI), which addresses sexual abuse in faith communities, and a member of the foundational board for the International Institute for Trauma and Addiction Professionals (IITAP), focusing on the development of the certification of sexual addiction therapists (CSAT). He currently serves on the executive council of the New Hope Educational Foundation.

Made in the USA
Thornton, CO
05/05/22 14:40:35